Silver Link Silk Editions

SLP

·W·
ALEXANDER
·& SONS, LTD·

Buses and Coaches
1955-1956

Henry Conn

Silver Link Silk Editions

SLP

W · ALEXANDER & SONS, LTD ·

BUSES AND COACHES
1955-1956

SLP

Silver Link Books

First published in 2020

British Library Cataloguing in Publication Data

A catalogue record for this book is available
from the British Library.

ISBN 978 1 85794 559 1

Silver Link Books
Mortons Media Group Limited
Media Centre
Morton Way
Horncastle
LN9 6JR
Tel/Fax: 01507 529535

email: sohara@mortons.co.uk
Website: www.mortonsbooks.co.uk

Printed and bound in the Czech Republic

Contents

Acknowledgements

Without kind permission from Robin Fell for access to the wonderful collection of Alexander buses and coaches negatives from 1955 onwards this book would not have been possible, so my sincere thanks.

I would also like to thank Stewart J. Brown who has very kindly written the foreword for this book, and for his amendments and comments on the draft – very much appreciated.

Foreword

In 1955-56 W. Alexander & Sons Ltd operated some 2,000 buses and coaches in an area that extended from Glasgow and Edinburgh in the south to Inverness and Aberdeen in the north. The company ran infrequent rural routes to villages and hamlets throughout that area, and intensive urban services in towns such as Falkirk, Stirling, Kirkcaldy, Dunfermline and Perth. In addition, its Bluebird coaches provided day and holiday coach tours from most of the towns within its vast operating territory.

It was a varied fleet, and Henry Conn has pulled together an impressive collection of photographs that capture that variety. None of the photographs have been published before, so they contain a few surprises even for those of us familiar with Alexander's buses. They are a reminder, too, of how the bus industry was changing. Most of the vehicles illustrated are traditional front-engined types; there are comparatively few of the then new mid-engined single-deckers that made up just over 10 per cent of the fleet by the summer of 1956.

This is an evocative and enjoyable journey through Alexander's operations in the middle of the 1950s.

Stewart J. Brown
Editor, *Buses Annual*
Largs, North Ayrshire

Introduction

Alexander's Motor Services of Kilsyth started operating in 1923, and W. Alexander & Sons Ltd was formed in 1924. In 1929 the company joined the SMT group of companies, but retained its independence and, by this time, was operating throughout much of Scotland.

Simultaneously with this expansion, Alexander had been building bus and coach bodies for its own use since its earliest operating days. From 1930 onwards this aspect of the business also expanded, and the company began to produce bodywork for other members of the SMT group, and later also for other companies. This enterprise was to become Walter Alexander & Co (Coachbuilders) Ltd in 1947.

The company's acquisition and expansion programme took a different turn in 1952, when all operations in the Inverness area were transferred to Highland Omnibuses. In 1961 the company, and its fleet of 2,000 vehicles, was reorganised into three areas: Fife, based in Kirkcaldy, Northern, based in Aberdeen, and Midland, based in Falkirk. Each subsequently acquired its own livery, with Fife being red and cream, Northern yellow and cream, and Midland blue and cream.

From 1934 onwards coaches were cream, or off-white, with variations of blue roofs and lining, and were given a 'Bluebird' emblem, which became synonymous with Alexander's coaching activities, even after the adoption of the new regional liveries in 1961.

Alexander vehicles were identified by a fleet number and a type prefix, for example 'C' for Commer, 'G' for Guy, 'W' for Bedford, and after the fleet was reorganised in 1961 a prefix of 'N' for Northern, 'F' for Fife and 'M' for Midland was added to the fleet number, e.g. C1 became NC1.

The photographs in this book were all taken in 1955 and 1956. On 24 February 1955 a big freeze across the UK resulted in many roads being blocked by snow – Caithness was practically cut off. The Royal Air Force worked to deliver food and medical supplies to the worst affected areas. On 21 March American evangelist Billy Graham began a seven-week Scottish crusade at the Kelvin Hall, Glasgow. On 1 April the South of Scotland Electricity Board was formed by merger, and on the 23rd the Scottish Cup Final was broadcast live on television for the first time – Clyde FC drew 1-1 with Celtic, winning the replay 1-0.

On 19 May the Greenock coin hoard was found, which contained around 60 Scottish coins dating from between 1543 and 1570. Eight days later the United Kingdom general election took place and in Scotland, as throughout the UK as a whole, the Conservatives had a majority of seats. On 30 June two Hawker Sea Hawk jet fighters flying from RNAS Lossiemouth independently crashed into the North Sea; one pilot was killed. At the end of July 1955 Operation 'Sandcastle' took place, when the first load of deteriorating captured Nazi German bombs filled with Tabun, a nerve agent, was shipped from Cairnryan on the SS *Empire Claire* for scuttling in the Atlantic Ocean. The first electricity supply to the isolated railway community at Riccarton Junction was connected on 30 September. A major fire in Edinburgh on 10 November destroyed the footwear warehouse of C. W. Carr Aitkman in Jeffrey Street. The next day a second major fire in Edinburgh largely destroyed the C&A fashion store in Princes Street. Cumbernauld was designated a New Town on 9 December, and five days later RMS *Carinthia* was launched at John Brown & Company's shipyard on Clydebank for the Cunard Line's Canadian service.

On 7 March 1956 the first floodlit Scottish Football League match was played at Ibrox Park in Glasgow between home team Rangers FC and Queen of the South; the score was 8-0. On 1 June Elsie Stephenson became the founding director of the Nurse Teaching Unit, University of Edinburgh, the first nurse teaching unit within a British university. On 4 July the National Library of Scotland's first purpose-built premises were opened on George IV Bridge in Edinburgh. On 29 July the Ecurie Ecosse motor racing team of Ninian Sanderson and Ron Flockhart won the 1956 24 Hours of Le Mans race.

On 14 August John Crichton-Stuart, 5th Marquess of Bute (born 1904) died and bequeathed the uninhabited islands of St Kilda to the National Trust for Scotland as a bird sanctuary. The TAT-1 transatlantic telephone cable between the UK and North America was inaugurated on 25 September; it came ashore near Oban. On 4 October the Prince's Cairn was unveiled at Loch nan Uamh to mark the spot where Charles Edward Stuart left Scotland in 1746 after the failure of the Jacobite rising of 1745.

Two tramways closed in 1956, Dundee on 20 October and Edinburgh on 16 November. In the 1956 Summer Olympics at Melbourne on 2 December, Richard McTaggart of Dundee won a gold medal in lightweight boxing. The Thurso lifeboat was destroyed on 10 December when its boathouse was burned out.

It is noteworthy that the average weekly wage in the UK in 1956 was just over £10 a week, the average house cost £2,150 and the average new car £720.

Famous people born in Scotland in 1955	
18 January	Robin Wales, Labour politician and mayor of London Borough of Newham
3 February	Kirsty Wark, television presenter
19 March	John Burnside, writer
31 March	Angus Young, rock musician
23 April	Allan Forsyth, footballer
2 May	Willie Miller, footballer
5 May	John Stroyan, Anglican bishop
14 May	Alasdair Fraser, fiddler
4 June	Val McDermid, crime novelist
13 June	Alan Hansen, footballer and television presenter
1 July	Candia McWilliam, fiction writer
8 July	Douglas Flint, banker
12 July	Robin Robertson, poet, novelist and editor
25 August	John McGeoch guitarist (died 2004 in England)
11 October	Sally Magnusson, journalist and broadcaster
12 October	Aggie MacKenzie, television presenter
28 October	Jeff Stewart, actor
12 November	Les McKeown, pop-rock singer

22 November	Mary Macmaster, harpist
2 December	Janice Galloway, writer
6 December	Anne Begg, Labour politician
23 December	Carol Ann Duffy, poet

Famous people born in Scotland in 1956	
7 January	Ian Bell, journalist (died 2015)
11 January	Phyllis Logan, actress
22 February	Philip Kerr, writer (died 2018)
25 February	Davie Cooper, footballer (died 1995)
19 April	Anne Glover, biologist
7 May	Calum MacDonald, Labour MP
7 September	Robert Reed, judge, Justice of Supreme Court of United Kingdom
26 September	Mick Imlah, poet (died 2009 in England)
3 November	Cathy Jamieson, Labour MP
29 December	Fred MacAulay, comedian

1955

Below: **KIRKCALDY** Our journey begins in Kirkcaldy on 18 April 1955. Indicating a journey to Dunfermline is No RB156 (DWG 912), an Alexander-bodied Leyland PD2/12 new in May 1953. At the time this view was taken this Leyland was allocated to Dunfermline D2 (Market Street); on 15 May 1961 it was transferred to W. Alexander & Sons (Midland) Limited, where it remained until its sale in June 1970.

Above: **DUNFERMLINE** on the same day is Leyland Service Vehicle No 125 (FG 6515). The NCME-bodied Guy Arab II is No RO718 (GYL 437), new to London Transport in December 1945 and acquired by Alexander in March 1953. Note that in 1955 the bus was part of the Perth City services fleet and has its indicator set for Cherrybank in Perth; as can be seen by the replacement panels on both upper and lower decks, the bodywork repairs must have been completed in Dunfermline rather than Perth. The Guy Arab ran in the red Perth City fleet from 1953 until its sale in June 1962 to Northern Roadways.

Above: **DUNFERMLINE** Also allocated to Dunfermline's Market Street depot was No K52 (WG 7490), an Alexander-bodied Leyland LZ2A new in June 1938. By the time this view was taken in Dunfermline on 19 April 1955, No K52 had been fitted with a Leyland 7.4-litre six-cylinder oil engine replacing the original six-cylinder petrol engine; the oil engine had been fitted in November 1946. No K52 was withdrawn in February 1958 and was acquired by the well-known independent operator Dunoon Motor Services in September of that year, where it remained until withdrawal in 1961. The route indicator is 306, Dunfermline to Leven via the coast with a journey time of 1 hour 50 minutes; the fare was 2s 6d single, 4s 9d return.

Right: **DUNFERMLINE** At the bus station on 19 April is No AC26 (FMS 982), a Park Royal-bodied AEC Monocoach new in October 1954. Interestingly, it is working a short journey to Crombie, a village 3 miles to the west of Dunfermline, but the garage code indicated is Stepps. During weekdays there was a service to Crombie every hour, taking 16 minutes at a fare of 5d. It may be that the conductor has stopped winding the destination blind to help the alighting passenger with his luggage. No AC26 was sold to a breaker in October 1970. The AEC Monocoach was produced by AEC between 1954 and 1957 and almost all were bodied by Park Royal or Alexander.

Opposite above right: **EDINBURGH** In St Andrew Square, indicating a journey to Stirling on 1 October 1955 is No PA191 (CWG 293), an Alexander coach-bodied Leyland PS1 new in June 1950. During weekdays a bus left Edinburgh for Stirling every 30 minutes on route 323, and on Saturdays this was increased to every 15 minutes and Sundays every 30 minutes. The journey time was 1 hour 53 minutes, and the single fare was 2s 9d. In the background is an SMT AEC Regent III. The Leyland PS1 remained in the Alexander Midland fleet until May 1970.

Above: **EDINBURGH** On 15 October we see No K35 (WG 7267), a Burlingham coach-bodied Leyland LZ2A new in July 1938. The original petrol engine fitted was replaced by an AEC 7.7-litre oil engine in April 1947. No K35 was acquired by Sowerby's Tours Ltd of Gilsland in March 1959 and scrapped in October 1960.

Above: **EDINBURGH** Standing behind No PA186 is No K65 (WG 7503), an Alexander-bodied Leyland LZ2A new in July 1938. The Alexander bodies of the Leyland LZ2As proved to be very heavy for the original petrol engines fitted, and No K65 was fitted with a Leyland 7.4-litre oil engine in April 1947. The vehicle was sold in April 1959.

Above: **EDINBURGH** On the same day we see No PA186 (CWG 288), an Alexander coach-bodied Leyland PS1 new in August 1950; it would pass to Alexander Midland in May 1961 and remain in that fleet until its sale in July 1970, later being noted with Shanks & McEwan as a staff bus in May 1972.

Right: **LARBERT** At Larbert depot on 30 October is (left) withdrawn Alexander-bodied Leyland LT5B No P281 (WG 2329). This bus Had been new to Alexander as No N133 in March 1934 and originally had a four-cylinder oil engine, which was replaced in January 1936 with a Leyland 8.6-litre oil engine. At that time the fleet number was changed from N133 to P281. The bus was transferred to David Lawson in June 1954 and was sold to a dealer a few days after this view was taken.

Alongside is No P156 (WG 2360), an Alexander-bodied Leyland LT5B new in July 1934, which passed to Lawson in July 1944 until August 1945. The Alexander bodywork was destroyed by fire in August 1945 and a new Burlingham body was fitted in September 1947. During 1953 No P156 returned to Lawson and remained in the fleet until April 1958, when it was scrapped.

Above: **LARBERT** Alexander acquired the business of J. Sutherland of Peterhead on 1 March 1950. Standing withdrawn in Larbert on 30 October (left) is No P859 (AV 9894), originally a Duple-bodied Leyland TS8 new in December 1937; its bodywork was significantly rebuilt at Falkirk in 1950. Alongside is another ex-Sutherland bus, No P857 (AV 8330), a Duple-bodied Leyland TS7 new in June 1936. No P857 passed to Fairclough of Wigan and was last licensed in December 1959; No P859 passed to MacKenzie of Motherwell and was last licensed in December 1960.

AboveRight: **LARBERT** Travelling to Falkirk on 30 October, this is No A100 (DMS 126), an Alexander-bodied AEC Regal III new in 1951 (its chassis was ordered by Sutherland of Peterhead). No A100 was one of a batch of six AEC Regals that were the last to be delivered new to Alexander and had the smaller AEC 7.7-litre engine with 8-foot-wide bodywork on a 7ft 6in chassis. All six passed to Alexander Northern in May 1961; No A100 was sold in March 1971.

Right: **LARBERT** At Larbert Road depot on 30 October is a line-up of Leyland Titans, the newest of which is nearest to the camera, No RB150 (DWG 906), an Alexander-bodied Leyland PD2/12 new in March 1953.

Above:: **GLASGOW** This view, together with the next six, was taken in Glasgow on 19 November 1955. During June 1954 Alexander started taking delivery of its first Alexander coach-bodied Leyland PSUC1/2s. Representing this delivery is No PD2 (FMS 719); in September 1972 it was noted as a staff bus with Robertson of Dumbarton.

Right: **GLASGOW** In Germiston Street, outside Buchanan Street bus station, is No AC22 (FMS 978), a Park Royal-bodied AEC Monocoach new in October 1954. Route 7 between Glasgow and Bo'ness was a very regular service, with buses leaving Buchanan Street at intervals of around 20 minutes; the journey time was 1 hour 40 minutes and a single fare to Bo'ness was 2s 8d. No AC22 was sold for scrap in September 1969. In the background is an SMT-bodied AEC Regent III.

Left **GLASGOW** Parked up in Cunningham Street, Glasgow, on the bridge above the tracks leaving Queen Street railway station, is Stepps-based No RA25 (AWG 363), a Leyland PD1 with Alexander bodywork new in February 1948; it would be sold to a dealer in December 1967.

Right: **GLASGOW** Just arrived at Dundas Street bus station is Lawson's No RO458 (AMS 45), a Guy Arab II originally with Roe bodywork but which received a new ECW body in June 1951. No RO458 passed to Alexander Midland in May 1961 and remained in the fleet until October 1965. All of Lawson's services used Dundas Street, and Alexander Midland continued these services until Dundas Street closed.

Left: **GLASGOW** Between August and October 1945 nine Leyland-bodied Leyland LT5As were acquired by Alexander via Millburn Motors of Glasgow; they were Nos VD 3411, VD 3414 and VD 3421 from Lanarkshire Traction, and Nos VD 3433, VD 3434, VD 3444, VD 3459, VD 3469 and VD 3471 from Central SMT. They were all rebodied by Alexander between October and December 1945, and also re-engined at that time. No P720 (VD 3469), seen here, was fitted with a Leyland 8.6-litre engine in October 1945 and was transferred to Lawson's in April 1954; it would remain in that fleet until July 1959, when it was sold for scrap.

Right: **GLASGOW** In this intriguing view of Dundas Street bus station, nearest the camera, leaving the bus station for Auchinairn, is Lawson's No RO450 (WG 9976), a Roe-bodied Guy Arab II new in October 1943. This bus was sold to Highland Omnibuses in May 1957 and sold for scrap in April 1958. To the right is Lawson's No RO449 (WG 9975), a Roe-bodied Guy Arab II new in August 1943; it would be sold to Highland Omnibuses in February 1956 and remain in that fleet until 1959.

Above: **GLASGOW** This view of Lawson's No P172 (WG 2376) was taken on the forecourt of Dundas Street bus station. Alexander took delivery of this vehicle in August 1934; a Leyland LT5B, it was originally bodied by Alexander, but received a Burlingham body in 1947. Lawson's acquired the bus in September 1953 and it remained in that fleet until sold in October 1959.

Above right: **CAMELON** This is No AC18 (FMS 765), one of a batch of 10 Park Royal-bodied AEC Reliances new in 1954, being the first to enter service with Alexander. Passing to Alexander Midland in May 1961, No AC18 was sold in October 1970. This view was taken in Brown Street, Camelon, outside the company's head office.

Right: **KELTY** On 26 November 1955 we start our journey in the Kingdom of Fife at Kelty. On 26 June 1950 Walter Alexander acquired the business of Wemyss Brothers of Ardersier, and this is No RO694 (BST 57), a Roe-bodied Guy Arab II that was new to Wemyss Brothers in May 1945; it remained in that fleet until sold to T. D. Alexander of Sheffield in June 1959.

Above: **KELTY** Also at Kelty depot is No P430 (WG 6419), an Alexander-bodied Leyland TS7 new in December 1937. A few of these survived the transfer to the three companies; unfortunately No P430 did not, being sold to a dealer in July 1959.

Above right: **LOCHGELLY** The business of Simpson's & Forrester's Limited of Dunfermline was taken over by Walter Alexander in February 1938, with a fleet of 69 buses dating from 1926 to 1937. Seen here at Lochgelly depot is (right) No P486 (FG 9430), an Alexander-bodied Leyland LT5B new to Simpson's & Forrester's in April 1934. It was fitted with a Leyland 8.6-litre oil engine in June 1939 and remained in the fleet until sold for scrap in January 1956.

Right: **LOCHGELLY** Also at the depot is No R353 (WG 3485), which began service life as an Alexander-bodied Leyland TS7 in July 1935 with fleet number No P261. It was rebuilt to Leyland TD4 specification and rebodied with a new Alexander L27/26 body in April 1943 and renumbered R353; the bus would be scrapped by Alexander in July 1957. The route indicated is 334, Lochgelly to Kirkcaldy, and during weekdays this route had a 20-minute headway. The journey time was 35 minutes, the single fare was 11d and the return 1s 10d.

Above: **LOCHGELLY** At the back of Lochgelly depot is No G40 (AMS 570), a Massey-bodied Guy Arab III new in August 1946 – I like the Massey bodywork. All 101 Guy Arab III single-deckers, numbered G1 to G101, were delivered with 5LW engines; the first 71 were coaches and the remaining 30 buses, bodied by the manufacturer. Twenty of the coaches received Massey bodywork, Nos G31 to G40 in 1946 and G62 to G71 in 1948. This bus passed to the Alexander Fife fleet on 15 May 1961 and remained there until sold in December 1965.

Above right: **COWDENBEATH** Seen heading for Burntisland on 26 November 1955 is No R553 (JY 5014), a Weymann-bodied Leyland TD4 new to Plymouth Corporation in 1935 and acquired by Alexander and renumbered in August 1945. Before entering service No R553 was fitted with a new Alexander L27/26 body and fitted with a Leyland 7.4-litre oil engine; the bus was scrapped by Alexander in June 1957.

Right: **KIRKCALDY** On the same day we have now travelled on to Kirkcaldy, and on the Esplanade is No RO677 (CAV 175), an NCME-bodied Guy Arab II new to Sutherland of Peterhead in December 1943. Route 308 was between Kirkcaldy and Leven, with a bus every 45 minutes and a journey time of 41 minutes. The single fare was 11d and the return 2s 0d. No RO677 passed to Alexander Fife on 15 May 1961 and was sold to the local scrap dealer Muir of Kirkcaldy in August 1962.

Right: **KIRKCALDY** At the Kirkcaldy depot of Alexander on the Esplanade is the very recently refurbished No PA115 (BWG 520), an Alexander-bodied Leyland PS1 new in March 1949. It was transferred to Alexander Midland at the splitting of the company, and was sold in May 1970; it was noted as staff transport with Unit Construction in July of that year.

Below right: **KIRKCALDY** At the front of the depot is No PA7 (AWG 542), an Alexander-bodied Leyland PS1 new in March 1947. This was one of the first Leyland PS1s to be delivered to Alexander, a total of 48 being delivered during 1947. On transfer to Alexander Fife, No PA7 was the oldest PS1 to be transferred and after sale was noted in 1968 at a farm in Coupar Angus being used as staff transport; it was out of service in 1977.

Below: **KIRKCALDY** Another company acquired by Alexander was the General Motor Carrying Company Limited of Kirkcaldy in May 1937. Seen on the Esplanade is one of the buses acquired, AFG 674, originally an Alexander-bodied Leyland TS7 new in June 1935. In June 1943 this bus had been rebuilt to TD4 specification with a new Alexander L26/26 body, given fleet number R375, and fitted with a Leyland 7.4-litre oil engine in December 1945; it was scrapped by Alexander in February 1958.

Below: **KIRKCALDY** Twenty Leyland OPS2/1s were built for export to New Zealand in 1948, but the order was changed to the OPS3 model. The 20 chassis were acquired by Alexander and remained in store until 1952. The OPS2 model had a 9.8-litre 'O.600' engine and an 8-foot-wide chassis, and the 20 eventually received 8-foot-wide Alexander bodywork with a length of 28ft 5in. Representative of this batch is No PB3 (DMS 816), new in January 1952; in 1960 it was converted to PS1 standard and was transferred to Alexander Fife in May 1961, remaining in the fleet until late 1970.

Above: **KIRKCALDY** Awaiting the scrapman at Kirkcaldy depot is (left) No R622 (BWE 40), a Cravens-bodied Leyland TD4 new to Sheffield Corporation in November 1935. Alongside is No R612 (AWB 942), a Cravens-bodied Leyland TD3 new to Sheffield Corporation in December 1934. Both buses had been acquired by Alexander in August 1947 and were sold a very short time after this view was taken.

Below: **KIRKALDY** This is an interesting view. Previously seen on the same day at Lochgelly on page 15, is No P486; it would appear this Leyland No P486 has made a journey to Kirkcaldy and, judging by the open bonnet, has broken down. As it was sold for scrap a few weeks after the date of this view, we can presume that the damage was not worth repairing.

Above **KIRKCALDY** The last view taken on 26 November 1955 is of No RO638 (HGC 185), a Weymann-bodied Guy Arab II new to London Transport in November 1945. This bus was acquired in November 1951, survived the company split in May 1961 and was sold for scrap in February 1963.

1956

FALKIRK It is 22 January 1956, and standing on the parking area near the town's bus station is No RA11 (AMS 11), an Alexander-bodied Leyland PD1 new in January 1948. This Larbert-allocated bus is destined for Fankerton, a village 6 miles north-west of Falkirk. On weekdays in 1956 there were 13 journeys to Fankerton from Falkirk bus station with a journey time of 30 minutes and a fare of 9d one way. No RA11 would remain in the Alexander Midland fleet until sold in January 1967.

FALKIRK In the bus station with no driver but quite a few passengers waiting to journey via Slamannan to Airdrie is No PA195 (BMS 315), an Alexander-bodied Leyland PS1 new in June 1950. On the left, also about to journey to Airdrie, is No AC8 (FMS 755), an Alexander-bodied AEC Reliance new in March 1955. In 1956 route 79 had 16 weekday journeys between Falkirk and Airdrie via Slamannan with a journey time of 50 minutes, while route 78 had ten weekday journeys between Falkirk and Airdrie via Allandale with a journey time of an hour. A single fare between Falkirk and Airdrie was 1s 7d. No PA195 would be sold in August 1969 and AC8 in June 1970.

Right: **FALKIRK** Back to the bus park, nearest the camera is No AB1 (BMS 110), a Burlingham-bodied AEC Regal I new in November 1947; it would be scrapped by Alexander Midland in July 1965. Alongside is No R259 (WG 8683), an all-Leyland TD5 new to Lawson's in June 1939; it passed to Alexander in November 1943, and to Alexander Midland in May 1961, being scrapped six months later.

Below: **FALKIRK** The camera has now moved back to give a panoramic view of the bus park. Nearest the camera is No AB1 (BMS 110), captioned in the previous view. Next in line now is No R284 (WG 9198), an all-Leyland TD7 new in March 1940. The next two in line are an Alexander-bodied Leyland PD1 and an Alexander-bodied Leyland PS1.

FALKIRK Indicating Bo'ness in Falkirk bus station is No AC16 (FMS 763), an Alexander-bodied AEC Reliance new in September 1954. This bus has been on the road for 1 hour 15 minutes from Buchanan Street, Glasgow, and will arrive in Bo'ness 25 minutes after leaving Falkirk. This bus was sold to Tiger of Salsburgh in November 1969.

Above: **LARBERT** is our next stop, on 22 January 1956, and the camera has captured No R253 (WG 8677), an all-Leyland TD5 new in June 1939. Route 91 was between Larbert and Laurieston, with four journeys per hour to Laurieston and a journey time of 30 minutes. No R253 would pass to Alexander Midland in May 1961 and was sold to a dealer four months later.

Above right: **LARBERT** Here is a good comparison of bus bodywork at Larbert depot, with 12 years between the two buses. Nearest the camera is No R317 (WG 9546), an all-Leyland TD7 new in February 1941. To the right is No RB150 (DWG 906), an Alexander-bodied Leyland PD2/12 new in March 1953. No R317 will be sold for scrap in November 1963, and No RB150 will be sold in October 1970.

Right: **FALKIRK** Back at Falkirk bus park, this is No RA18 (AWG 356), an Alexander-bodied Leyland PD1 new in January 1948. The indicated route 83B was between Grangemouth and Maddiston via Falkirk bus station, with a journey time of around 35 minutes. In 1945 Leyland announced for delivery the following year a brand-new Titan, with only the front axle being similar to that of the TD7. Among the new features was the E181 7.4-litre engine. The PD1 range ceased to be catalogued at the end of 1947, replaced by the PD2, which had been announced at the end of 1946. No RA18 would be sold in November 1967.

Above: **FALKIRK** This is No PA135 (CMS 203), an Alexander-bodied Leyland PS1 new in July 1949.

Above right: **FALKIRK** In the town's bus station is No AB6 (BMS 115), a Burlingham-bodied AEC Regal III new in October 1947. It was sold in April 1965 and passed to a showman four months later.

Right: **LARBERT** Back at Larbert on 22 January, nearest the camera is No R333 (WG 9642), an all-Leyland TD7 new in March 1942. To the right is No R314 (WG 9543), an all-Leyland TD7 new in January 1941. The only detail changes that I can see in this view are the driver's mirror and the lack of a black wheel mudguard on No R314, possibly due to accident damage; both buses would be sold in 1963.

Below: **LARBERT** Also seen at the depot is No R319 (WG 9547), an all-Leyland TD7 new in January 1941 and sold to Bellshill & Mossend Scrap Metal Company in February 1964. The TD7 was the final pre-war Titan and, built with the TD5, it had a flexible engine mounting and a larger flywheel. Most of them and some late TD5s were frozen in production by Government order with the fall of France in May 1940, then in late 1941 the TD5 and TD7 stocks were 'unfrozen' and finished, so that the Titan line could be closed for war production.

Above: **EDINBURGH** The date is 10 March 1956 and the trams in Edinburgh still have a few more months of operation. On Princes Street in service to Callander is No PD65 (GWG 291), an Alexander-bodied Leyland PSUC1/2 new in January 1956; its depot plate is 'Bn', so it is working out of Bannockburn depot. Every hour from St Andrew Square during weekdays a bus would leave for Callander with a journey time of 2 hours 50 minutes and a single fare of 4s 1d. This bus would be the last standing of the 1955 buses transferred to Alexander Midland in May 1961, and was sold in August 1972.

DUNFERMLINE Unloading passengers at the town's bus station on 11 March 1956 is No P543 (WG 8122), an Alexander-bodied Leyland TS8 new in May 1939. By April 1961 this bus had been converted to a service lorry and was transferred to Alexander Fife a month later. Renumbered L5, the lorry was withdrawn in 1978.

Above: **DUNFERMLINE** This rather smoky bus is No G88 (BMS 858), an all-Guy Arab III new in February 1948. The Gardner 5LW engine fitted to it was a reconditioned unit from a Guy Arab II, which received a Gardner 6LW as a replacement; despite the amount of exhaust being omitted by No G88 on this day, it would remain in the fleet until December 1965.

Above right: **INVERKEITHING** On the Dunfermline service on 11 March 1956 is No RO602 (AWG 388), a Cravens-bodied Guy Arab III new in May 1948. The journey time between Inverkeithing and Dunfermline was 20 minutes and the single fare was 5d. No RO602 would be sold to Muir of Kirkcaldy in November 1969.

Right: **DUNFERMLINE** In April 1934 Simpson's & Forrester's of Dunfermline took delivery of an Alexander-bodied Leyland LT5B (FG 9432). In February 1938 Alexander acquired the business and the Leyland was renumbered P488. In April 1955 the bodywork was scrapped by Alexander and the chassis became lorry No L185, fitted with a body in June 1955; it was transferred to Alexander Fife in May 1961 and sold for scrap to Muir in May 1965. This view was taken in Dunfermline on 11 March 1956.

Right: **DUNFERMLINE** A few yards away is No PA76 (BWG 302), an Alexander-bodied Leyland PS1 new in 1948.

Far right: **MURRAYFIELD** Seen on 17 March 1956 is No PA204 (CWG 331), a Burlingham-bodied Leyland PS1 new in July 1950. It was transferred to Alexander Northern in May 1961 and remained in the fleet until June 1971, when it was sold to Farquhar of Aberdeen as a staff bus, remaining there for just under three years before being scrapped.

Right: **MURRAYFIELD** On 17 March 1956 Scotland played host to England at rugby, and unfortunately lost 6-11. A large number of buses were used to transport supporters from all over Scotland and England, and at Murrayfield is (centre) No PA79 (BWG 305), an Alexander-bodied Leyland PS1 new in July 1948. To the left is SX 7007, a Duple-bodied Bedford OB new to McLucas of South Queensferry in 1950, and seen here owned by J. P. Hardie. To the right is XHN 49, a Duple-bodied Bedford SBG new in 1955 to Percival of Richmond.

Above: **MURRAYFIELD** Next to No PA204 is Western SMT No AL615 (CSD 21), an Alexander-bodied Leyland PS1 new in 1950; the 'A' code signifies that the vehicle is allocated to Ayr depot. It remained in the fleet until purchased by Rockfall of Middlesbrough in March 1966; it was later noted with McKean of Glasgow by September 1967.

Above right: **TYNECASTLE** It is 31 March 1956, and Heart of Midlothian are at home to Dunfermline in the Scottish League Division 1 – the score was 5-0 to Hearts. Seen here is No PA77 (BWG 303), an Alexander-bodied Leyland PS1.

Right: **TYNECASTLE** The Leyland TS8 was revised with a shorter bonnet to become the TS8 special. SMT and Alexander especially favoured this type, as it could seat 39 rather than 35 in the 27ft 6in maximum length allowed for two-axle single deckers. Here we see No P580 (WG 8807), an Alexander-bodied Leyland TS8 special new in June 1939; it was sold in December 1961 and noted as a showman's vehicle in Kirkcaldy in April 1962.

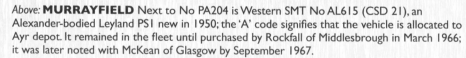

Above: **TYNECASTLE** The third view at Tynecastle on that day shows No W201 (AWG 992), an SMT-bodied Bedford OB new in June 1947. In 1946 Alexander began to purchase the more comfortable and less restricted Bedford OB when it came back into production, and a total of 43 OB coaches joined the fleet between 1946 and 1950, numbered W192-223, W229-238 and W240. The majority were bodied by SMT to the Duple Vista design, but with one easily visible modification: SMT examples had the entry doors sliding inside the sidewall, whereas Duple examples were outside. No W201 was transferred to Alexander Midland in May 1961 and sold in April 1963.

Above right: **EDINBURGH** A total of five Strachan-bodied Albion FT3ABs were purchased by Alexander in May and June 1950 and they served their entire working lives in Fife. In Edinburgh on 1 April 1956 is No BA2 (CWG 227), which would be withdrawn and sold for scrap in July 1964.

Right: **BURNTISLAND** En route to Leven on 4 April 1956 is No R374 (WG 3453). This bus was originally an Alexander-bodied Leyland TS7 new in June 1935, then in June 1943 it was rebuilt to TD4 specification and received a new Alexander L27/26 body; it was withdrawn and sold in January 1957. Route 306 was between Dunfermline and Leven with two buses per hour on Monday to Saturday. The journey time was 1 hour 50 minutes, and from Burntisland this bus has just over an hour to arrive at Leven. The single fare between Dunfermline and Leven was 2s 6d.

Left: **BURNTISLAND** On the same day, with an indicator setting to Kelty, this is No R128 (WG 4930), an all-Leyland TD4 new in December 1936. It was scrapped by Alexander in March 1959.

Below left: **BURNTISLAND** The final view taken in this Fife town on that April day is of No RB74 (CWG 52), an Alexander-bodied Leyland PD2/1 new in May 1950. This bus is working route 310 between Burntisland and Upper Largo via Kirkcaldy. On Monday to Saturday the route had two buses per hour and a journey time of 1 hour 23 minutes. No RB74 passed to Alexander Fife in May 1961 and to Muir in March 1971.

Below: **EDINBURGH** On 5 April 1956 we see No D7 (BMS 402), a Burlingham-bodied Daimler CVD6 new in March 1948. Alexander acquired 35 half-cab Daimler CVD6 coaches during 1947-49, Nos D1-D35, and a further 13 full-front coaches in 1951, Nos D36-D48. All the half-cabs received Burlingham C33F bodies, and the majority served until 1965; No D7 was purchased by Highland Omnibuses in June 1965, then sold to Bruce of Ellon in October 1966.

Above: **DUNDEE** All the following views in Dundee were taken on 16 April 1956. In December 1949 the Dundee services of SMT were transferred to Alexander, and this included a fleet of more than 50 Alexander-bodied Leyland single-deck buses. This is No K100 (BSC 510), an Alexander-bodied Leyland LZ2A new in June 1938; it was acquired by Dunoon Motor Services in April 1958, remaining there until December 1961.

Above right: **DUNDEE** This is No K93 (BSC 503), another of the Alexander-bodied Leyland LZ2As, this one new to SMT in May 1937. This vehicle was also acquired by Dunoon Motor Services, in July 1958, and remained there until it was sold in May 1962.

Right: **DUNDEE** This is No P633 (WG 8112), an Alexander-bodied Leyland TS8 new in April 1939. The indicator is set for route 157, Dundee to Kirriemuir, which had a journey time of 55 minutes and a one-way fare of 1s 9d. No P633 passed to Alexander Northern on 15 May 1961 and was sold for scrap in October 1963.

DUNDEE Being readied for service to Tealing, a village 6 miles north of Dundee, is No P812 (ASF 369), an Alexander-bodied Leyland TS7 new in June 1937. A journey between Dundee and Tealing would take 18 minutes and the single journey fare was 8d. No P812 was sold to Buckley of Leith, a showman, in early 1957, and was last licensed in November 1961.

DUNDEE In the background of this view are the buildings of Thomas Justice & Sons, furniture-makers founded in 1872 in Tally Street, Dundee. The main showroom for carpets and furniture opened at Whitehall Street in 1892, and at its peak the business included ironmongery, upholstery, bedding, soft furnishings, electrical contractors, tiles and fireplaces. Later the firm branched into educational furnishings and shopfitting, but closed in 2004. No P619 (WG 9012) is an Alexander-bodied Leyland TS8 special that was new in March 1940; it passed to Alexander Northern in May 1961 and was scrapped in December 1963.

Above: **DUNDEE** Closer to the buildings of Thomas Justice & Sons is No RA58 (BWG 103), an Alexander-bodied Leyland PD1 new in July 1948. This bus has completed a journey on route 19B between Perth, Tay Street, and Dundee, North Tay Street, which had a journey time of 1 hour and a single fare of 2s 1d. No RA58 had a long service life, not being sold for scrap until October 1970.

Above right: **DUNDEE** On the city's cobbled streets is No PB6 (DMS 819), an Alexander coach-bodied Leyland OPS2/1 new in December 1951. Nos PB2, PB6, PB10 and PB11 were converted to PS1 standard in 1960, and four of the PB class were transferred to Alexander Northern in May 1961. This example was sold in March 1971.

Right: **DUNDEE** New in December 1949 was No PA144 (CMS 213), an Alexander-bodied Leyland PS1. It has completed a journey on route 11 from Aberdeen, which had a journey time of 3 hours 23 minutes; the single fare was 6s 7d and the return 12s 0d. No PA144 was withdrawn in 1960 and parts from it were taken and fitted to a new Alexander frame classified as Leyland PD3/3C No RB258 (RMS 690), which entered service in March 1961.

DUNDEE In this view just a few yards further down the street we see No A45 (AWG 632), an Alexander-bodied AEC Regal I new in August 1947. It was sold to Hill of Comrie in July 1967.

DUNDEE Muirhead is on the outskirts of Dundee on the A923 Coupar Angus Road. Route 150 was between Dundee and Auchterhouse village, and therefore No P822 (CSF 244) is on a short journey of that route, taking 15 minutes to get to Muirhead at a fare of 7d. This ex-SMT bus, an Alexander-bodied Leyland TS8, was new in April 1939. Like many Alexander buses, it would later become a staff bus for farmers in the Angus area, being acquired by Angus Seed Growers of Forfar; it was last licensed in November 1961.

DUNDEE Another Alexander-bodied Leyland TS8 is seen here, No P816 (CSF 224), which was new to SMT in April 1939. It has completed a journey on route 154 from Brechin to Dundee with a journey time of 1 hour 22 minutes, with a one-way fare of 2s 11d. No P816 would be sold to Mountain Transport Ltd of London SW3 in August 1957 and was last licensed by that company in December 1960.

DUNDEE With the tracks of the city's tram system in the foreground, this is No A40 (AWG 627), an Alexander-bodied AEC Regal I new in May 1947; it would pass to Alexander Northern in May 1961, and was then acquired by a contractor in Aberdeen in May 1968. The Dundee trams had just over six months left when this view was taken, the system closing on 20 October 1956.

DUNDEE New in March 1940 was No R290 (WG 9204), an all-Leyland TD7. It has completed a journey on route 11D from Monifieth to Dundee, which took 25 minutes for a single fare of 9d. Already more than 21 years old, No R290 passed to Alexander Northern in May 1961, where it remained until sold to a dealer in Aberdeen in February 1963.

Right: **ABERDOUR** The next five views were taken at Aberdour railway station on 10 June 1956. On the left is Stepps-allocated No RA25 (AWG 363), an Alexander-bodied Leyland PD1 new in February 1948; it was transferred to Alexander Midland in May 1961 and sold for scrap in December 1967. Alongside is SMT No H58 (FS 5580), a Leyland TS6 new in 1933 and rebodied with a Burlingham coach body in 1949. There is another view of RA25 in Glasgow on page 12.

Above: **KIRKCALDY** On 6 December 1947 a fleet of 20 buses was acquired from W. Greig of Inverness; 16 of them had been withdrawn by 1955, and only four Guy Arab IIs remained. In front of the Kirkcaldy depot on the Esplanade on 16 April 1956 is No RO570 (BST 31), an NCME-bodied Guy Arab II that had been new to Greig in February 1945; it operated on the Kirkcaldy town services in red livery until being sold to Muir of Kirkcaldy in November 1966.

Right: **COWDENBEATH** Route 315 ran two buses an hour every weekday between Cowdenbeath and Kirkford, with a journey time of 10 minutes. This is No RO716 (GYE 84), a Park Royal-bodied Guy Arab II that had been new to London Transport in July 1945. Alexander acquired the bus in March 1953 and it remained in stock until it was sold to a showman in Glasgow in July 1959.

Right: **ABERDOUR** This is No A71 (BMS 105), a Burlingham-bodied AEC Regal I new in September 1947 and in this view allocated to Grangemouth depot. It was sold in August 1965.

Below: **ABERDOUR** Another Grangemouth-allocated bus is No P598 (WG 8991), an Alexander-bodied Leyland TS8 special new in March 1940. Just after its transfer to Alexander Midland it was sold by Cruden in Musselburgh. In the background is one of the 1952 SMT Burlingham-bodied Bedford SBs.

Right: **ABERDOUR** On the left is No R116 (WG 4470), an all-Leyland TD4 new in November 1936. The bus was originally licensed to Falkirk & District Traction Company, but operated in Alexander livery until sold for scrap in December 1959. During 1949 Alexander took delivery of a batch of Commer Commandos bodied by Scottish Aviation of Prestwick, and representing this batch on the right is No C18 (CMS 290); only eight of the batch survived as far as the Alexander split in May 1961, including this one, and all were withdrawn in 1963.

Right: **CROOK OF DEVON** Heading for Alloa on 11 June 1956 is No P633 (WG 9323), an Alexander-bodied Leyland TS8 special new in May 1940. Route 40 was an infrequent service between Kinross Green's Hotel and Alloa bus station. The journey time was 1 hour 4 minutes, and No P633 would take 38 minutes to journey from Crook of Devon to Alloa. A single fare for the whole journey was 1s 10d.

Above: **BURNTISLAND** Less than a year into service is No AC79 (GWG 483), an Alexander-bodied AEC Monocoach showing a depot allocation of 'S' for Stirling; when Alexander split this coach passed to Alexander Northern and remained in that fleet until sold in October 1975.

Above: **BURNTISLAND** On 15 June a number of coaches are parked on the northern shore of the Firth of Forth, and their passengers will hopefully be sampling the excellent sandy beach here. On the right No D43 (DMS 558) is an ECW-bodied Daimler CVD6 new in June 1951, which passed to Alexander Midland in May 1961 and was sold for scrap in October 1965.

Right: **BURNTISLAND** This picture provides an interesting comparison of three Alexander-bodied Leyland coaches. On the left is No PA135 (CMS 203), new in 1949, which would be the donor of parts to No RB255 (RMS 687) in 1961. In the centre is No P395 (WG 5534), a Leyland TS7 new in April 1937 and sold in November 1960. On the right is No PC78 (EMS 533), a Leyland PSU1/15 new in April 1953; it was transferred to Alexander Midland in May 1961 and sold ten years later.

Above: **BURNTISLAND** The last coach captured by the camera at Burntisland on that day is No PD18 (FMS 735), an Alexander-bodied Leyland PSUC1/2 new in July 1954. The car behind is a Hillman Minx Mark VI, with a registration – FMS 792 – similar to the coach.

Above right: **MONTROSE** Looking smart in the town's depot on 2 August 1956 is No W221 (BWG 42), an SMT-bodied Bedford OB new in June 1948. This Bedford OB was the last to remain in service with Alexander Northern and was sold to Hay of Skene in August 1964 for use as a mobile shop.

Right: **DUNDEE** Parked in Leonard Street on 1 August 1956 is No W244 (EMS 827), a Burlingham-bodied Bedford SB new in May 1953. Highland Omnibuses later acquired the coach in December 1966, but decided not to use it and sold it to W. J. Sutherland of Glenbrittle. A. & C. McLennan of Spittalfield acquired the Bedford in June 1969 and it was scrapped by them by 1974.

MONTROSE The views in Montrose were all taken on 2 August 1956, and about to depart for Aberdeen on that day is No A49 (AWG 636), an Alexander-bodied AEC Regal I new in June 1947. Behind, also running to Aberdeen, is No R364 (SN 7139), originally a Martin-bodied Leyland TS7 new to Lawson of Kirkintilloch in May 1936. This bus was acquired by Alexander in May 1943, rebuilt to TD4 specification and fitted with a new Alexander L27/26 body, entering service in late May 1943; it was withdrawn and sold to a showman in December 1960.

Left: **MONTROSE** At the bus stance in the High Street is No A80 (BMS 466), an Alexander-bodied AEC Regal I new in January 1948. To the left is No R393, originally an Alexander-bodied Leyland TS7 new in July 1935; it was rebuilt to Leyland TD4 specification and rebodied with a new Alexander L27/26 body in September 1943. The bus to the right is a Rochdale-registered AEC Regal, new in 1931. Route 11 was between Aberdeen and Dundee, but my thoughts are that No A80 has worked a short route 11 between Arbroath and Montrose, which had a journey time of 38 minutes and a single fare of 1s 5d. No R393 is working route 44, the Montrose Circular to Brechin, Edzell, Aerodrome, Fettercairn, Laurencekirk, Marykirk, Hillside and back to Montrose, with a journey time of 1 hour 42 minutes.

Right: **DUNDEE** In the High Street is Dundee-allocated No R45 (WG 3379), an all-Leyland TD4 new in March 1935; it was scrapped by Alexander in June 1959.

Left: **DUNDEE** The statue in the High Street is of doctor and politician Joseph Hume, born in Montrose in 1777. Beside the statue is No P359 (WG 5496), an Alexander-bodied Leyland TS7 new in March 1937. It became a showman's bus in January 1961 and was sold for scrap by Alexander Northern in December 1963. On the left, No P613 (WG 9006) is an Alexander-bodied Leyland TS8 special new in March 1940.

Below left: **MONTROSE** The Church in the background is Montrose Old Church dating from 1791, with a steeple completed in 1834. A few passengers have boarded No P401 (WG 5919), an Alexander-bodied Leyland TS7 new in April 1937, which will be leaving soon for Dundee. Montrose to Dundee by route 11 took 1 hour 37 minutes and the fare was 3s 0d for a single journey. Note that the bus behind, No P407 (WG 5925), another Alexander-bodied Leyland TS7, is also indicated for Dundee; both passed to Alexander Northern in May 1961.

Right: **MONTROSE** With a goodly load of passengers, No P406 (WG 5924), an Alexander-bodied Leyland TS7 new in April 1937, is soon to depart for Aberdeen. Montrose to Aberdeen by route 11 took 1 hour 42 minutes and the single fare was 3s 9d. Just behind is an Aberdeen-registered Alvis TA14; this 'woody' dates from 1950.

STONEHAVEN We now travel 24 miles north to Stonehaven, where these views were taken on 3 August 1956. Outside Alexander's bus depot is No K55 (WG 7493), an Alexander-bodied Leyland LZ2A new in July 1938. The bus's original petrol engine was replaced by a Leyland 7.4-litre oil engine in September 1947. No K55 was sold for scrap in January 1959.

Above: **STONEHAVEN** Between July and November 1945 Alexander acquired from Plymouth Corporation one Leyland TD3 and 11 TD4s with Weymann bodywork. This is No R550 (JY 6737), a TD4 new in December 1935. It retained its original bodywork although it was heavily rebuilt at Aberdeen workshops; it subsequently passed to Alexander Midland in May 1961, but it is likely that it was never operated as it passed to a dealer in September of that year.

Above right: **STONEHAVEN** Alone is No RA55 (BWG 100), an Alexander-bodied Leyland PD1 new in September 1948. It passed to Alexander Midland in May 1961.

Righte: **STONEHAVEN** The conductress is having a word with the driver, possibly about the nondescript destination screen. Going somewhere 'special' is No P406 (WG 5924), an Alexander-bodied Leyland TS7 new in April 1937. The previous day this bus was in Montrose bound for Aberdeen!

STONEHAVEN Leaving for the 50-mile-plus trip to Dundee is Dundee-allocated No P620 (WG 9013), an Alexander coach-bodied Leyland TS8 special new in March 1940. It was sold for scrap by Alexander Northern in December 1963.

STONEHAVEN This is No 173 (CWG 275), an Alexander-bodied Leyland PS1 new in August 1950. It would be sold to Just Buses in March 1971, acquired by Harry's of Cheltenham in June 1972, then, through a dealer, sold to Lefevre of Oldham by August 1973.

Below: **STONEHAVEN** The final view taken here is of No PA171 (CWG 273), an Alexander-bodied Leyland PS1 new in August 1950. Happily it would be sold for preservation in June 1971.

Above: **STONEHAVEN** Another Leyland LZ2A allocated to Stonehaven in August 1956 is No K76 (WG 7514), new in June 1939. This coach was original fitted with a Leyland petrol engine, which was replaced by a Leyland 7.4-litre oil engine in 1947. No K76 was acquired by J. & J. Leith of Sanquhar in October 1957 and was noted derelict at that operator's premises in September 1962.

HUNTLY Later that day we have travelled the 40-plus miles to Huntly, where we see locally based No W71 (WG 8613), a Duple-bodied Bedford WTB new in April 1939. This vehicle and No W72 were the last Bedford WTBs to be withdrawn from service in 1957; No W71 was acquired by Dod Sims Garage in Aberdeen in February 1957 and became a mobile shop in Aberdeen a month later. The Commercial Bank of Scotland was founded in Edinburgh way back in 1810 surviving until 1958 when it merged with the National Bank of Scotland, which in turn became part of the Royal Bank of Scotland in 1968.

KEITH Just outside the town and heading for Elgin on 5 August 1956 is No P526 (WG 8105), an Alexander-bodied Leyland TS8 new in June 1939. By April 1960 it was owned by Sir Robert Fossett's Circus, and was still owned by them in July 1966.

Below: **BUCKIE** At the town's Alexander depot is No W215 (BMS 99), an SMT-bodied Bedford OB new in February 1948. This coach was allocated to Huntly and was one of the few OBs to transfer to Alexander Northern in May 1961; it was sold to Dundee Corporation Water Department in July 1962.

Above: **BUCKIE** is just over 12 miles from Keith, and this view was taken on 6 August 1956. This is No K4 (SN 8450), an Alexander-bodied Leyland LZ2A new to Lawson of Kirkintilloch in April 1938. The original petrol engine was replaced with a Leyland 7.4-litre oil engine in April 1947. During 1953 No K4 was withdrawn by Lawson and sold to Alexander, entering service in August 1953. It was sold to a dealer in April 1958, then passed to Mercury Coaches of Boscombe, where it remained until July 1959.

BUCKIE Passengers board No P388 (WG 5527), an Alexander-bodied Leyland TS7 new in April 1937, for the 17-mile journey to Elgin. This bus passed to Alexander Northern in May 1961 and, through Ross of Aberdeen, passed to Chisholm, a contractor in Edinburgh, for staff transport. Behind No P388 is a Burlingham-bodied AEC Regal I new in 1947, possibly BMS 100.

ELGIN All the views here were taken on 6 August 1956. Leaving the town's bus station is No A20 (AMS 495), a Burlingham-bodied AEC Regal I new in July 1946. It is heading for two destinations, Birnie and Roseisle; the Elgin to Birnie journey took 15 minutes and cost 6d for a single journey.

ELGIN Burlingham-bodied Daimler CVD6 No D12 (BMS 407) was delivered to Alexander in February 1948. Only four of these 30 vehicles passed to Alexander Northern in May 1961, and all four, including No D12, remained in the Northern fleet until 1970. Note in the background that the fair is in town.

Left: **ELGIN** In June 1950 there was a further revision to the Construction & Use Regulations: 8-foot-wide buses no longer required special permission and the maximum length for double-deckers was increased to 27 feet. Leyland raised a new set of variant codes for the PD2, these having a wheelbase of 16ft 5in. This is No RB163 (DWG 919), a Leyland PD2/12 new in June 1953, 8 feet wide and fitted with vacuum brakes. Only four PD2/12s passed to Alexander Northern, Nos RB161 to RB164 (DWG 917 to 920); No RB163 was exported to Sweden in April 1975.

Right: **ELGIN** Indicating Burghead, about 9 miles north-west of Elgin, and carrying a good number of passengers is No RA50 (BWG 95), an Alexander-bodied Leyland PD1 new in July 1948. Route 31 from New Elgin to Burghead via Elgin bus station was a frequent service with a journey time of 32 minutes between Elgin bus station and Burghead, with a single fare of 1 shilling. No RA50 was sold by Alexander Northern in October 1969.

ELGIN Originally fitted with a Leyland petrol engine, No K73 (WG 7511), an Alexander-bodied Leyland LZ2A, received a Leyland 7.4-litre oil engine in 1947. This vehicle was one of the last Leyland LZ2As to be delivered to Alexander in June 1939, and was sold to Kinnear Moodie, a contractor in Glasgow, in October 1958.

ELGIN Based in Elgin was No 132 (WG 9263), a Chevrolet 40-60cwt lorry new in 1939. It was sold to Finlay of Falkirk in August 1958.

ABERDEEN The following views in the 'Granite City' were taken on 8 and 9 August 1956. The Walter Alexander depot in Aberdeen was in Gairn Terrace, and nearest the camera is No W241 (EMS 824), one of a batch of 12 Burlingham-bodied Bedford SBs new between May and July 1953. At the time this view was taken the Bedford was allocated to Crieff depot; it was sold to a dealer in November 1966 and was noted on a farm in Lurgan, Northern Ireland, in September 1968.

Left: **ABERDEEN** Alongside one of the fuel pumps at Gairn Terrace is No P360 (WG 5497), an Alexander-bodied Leyland TS7 new in March 1937. It is indicating route 14, Aberdeen to Lumphanan, with five journeys each weekday and Saturday with three journeys on Sunday. The journey time to Lumphanan 1 hour 15 minutes and a single journey fare was 2s 6d. No P360 was sold for scrap in January 1960.

Right: **ABERDEEN** In Gairn Terrace, with the depot on the other side of the wall, is No PB11 (DMS 824), an Alexander-bodied Leyland OPS2/1 that entered service in January 1952. It was later acquired by Mitchell of Kinpurnie in June 1971.

ABERDEEN This is No A32 (AWG 619), an Alexander-bodied AEC Regal I new in August 1947. Thirty-four of the 1947 Alexander-bodied Regal Is passed to Alexander Northern in May 1961, and No A32 was among the last withdrawn in January 1968, later becoming a showman's bus in Inverness in August 1968.

ABERDEEN In a rare view, this is No AC95 (HMS 244), an Alexander-bodied AEC Reliance newly delivered to Alexander in Aberdeen. To the right is No R29 (WG 772), an all-Leyland TD2 that had been new in February 1932; it had been involved in an accident in May 1956 and would be scrapped by Alexander in April of the following year.

ABERDEEN Working a local tour is No PD10 (FMS 727), an Alexander coach-bodied Leyland PSUC1/2T new in July 1954. This vehicle was sold to Conway Hunt, Ottershaw, in August 1972, passed to Blue Line, Upminster, in January 1973, and a month later passed to Gray of Wootton Bassett.

ABERDEEN Montrose-based No P621 (WG 9014), an Alexander-bodied Leyland TS8 special new in March 1940, is destined for a journey to Brechin; leaving Dee Street in Aberdeen the journey to Brechin would take 5 minutes short of 2 hours and the single fare would cost 3s 11d, the return costing 7s 7d. On the left, leaving for Edinburgh is Stirling-based No PC20 (CMS 386), an Alexander coach-bodied Leyland PSU1/15 new in June 1952; it would pass to Alexander Midland in May 1961.

Right: **ABERDEEN** Working a tour is No PB10 (DMS 823), an Alexander coach-bodied Leyland OPS2/1 that entered service in January 1952. All the OPS2/1s had the 9.8-litre O600 engine and most served Alexander for around 20 years. This vehicle was sold in February 1972.

Left: **ABERDEEN** Stonehaven-based No P361 (WG 5498), an Alexander-bodied Leyland TS7 new in March 1937, will soon be making the long journey to Dundee. The journey time was 3 hours 23 minutes, for a single fare of 6s 7d, and a return the rather expensive 12s 0d. After withdrawal in 1960, No P361 became a showman's bus with Shand of Kinghorn, and five years later was with another showman, Walsh of Aberdeen. Note the billboard on the left for The Great Keith Show on 14 August 1956, with a 'grand display of livestock' and £2,000 in prize money.

ABERDEEN With the destination display set for a journey to its home depot of Stonehaven, this is No K70 (WG 7508), an Alexander-bodied Leyland LZ2A new in July 1938; by the time of this view it was fitted with a Leyland 7.4-litre oil engine. It would be sold a little over a year later and was taken to J. & J. Leith of Sanquhar, who later scrapped the chassis and transferred the body to KSM 40, a Crossley, in October 1962. Route 38A was from Aberdeen Dee Street via the Banchory/Devenick crossroads, Netheley Smithy and Stonehaven, with a journey time of 1 hour and a single fare of 1s 7d. Note the Music Hall billboard advertising the Tanner Sisters and Margery Manners. The Tanner Sisters made hundreds of appearances on radio, TV and music hall, even performing in 1958 with Buddy Holly. Actress Margery Manners never attained true top-of-the-bill status, but was ever popular with the audiences of music halls.

Left: **ABERDEEN** This is No P171 (CWG 273), an Alexander-bodied Leyland PS1 new in August 1950 and sold into preservation in June 1971. Monday to Friday every hour between 6.35am and 5.35pm a bus would leave Aberdeen for Inverness on Route 5. The journey time was 6 hours 9 minutes, a single fare was 11s 4d, and you would need just over a quid for the return. Alongside is Stonehaven-based K55 (WG 7493), an Alexander-bodied Leyland LZ2A new in July 1938 and withdrawn in November 1958. Appearing at the Beach Ballroom is Gracie Cole, who played cornet, with her own all-female band, which she fronted between 1952 and 1956 performing jazz and pop.

Left: **ABERDEEN** This is Burlingham coach-bodied No D19 (BMS 414) new in March 1948 and sold into preservation just over 22 years later.

ABERDEEN In the background of this view is the central brick spire of the three separate Free Churches, East, High and South. Indicating Tarland, a village 30 miles west of Aberdeen, is No P385 (WG 5524), an Alexander-bodied Leyland TS7 new in April 1937. On weekdays route 15 to Tarland had two buses per day, at 10.00am and 6.00pm, with a journey time of 1 hour 35 minutes, a single fare of 3s 1d and a return of 6s 1d. No P385 passed to a showman in 1960 and was scrapped in May 1964. Behind is No P384 (WG 5523), another 1937 Alexander-bodied Leyland TS7, which passed to Alexander Northern in May 1961 and was one of the last TS7s to be withdrawn early in 1963.

ABERDEEN Even in August long coats are still worn, although the flat caps are missing. This is Montrose-based No PA91 (BWG 317), an Alexander-bodied Leyland PS1 new in August 1948.

ABERDEEN This is No P530, an Alexander-bodied Leyland TS8 new in June 1939; it was acquired by a showman in April 1960. Note the Austin FX3 taxi in the right background, which was produced between 1948 and 1958.

ABERDEEN My mother and father had friends who lived in Dyce and I recall on many occasions taking the Corporation bus from Mastrick to connect with an Alexander bus to Dyce. If at all possible I would dash upstairs, along the sunken gangway and seat myself on the front bench seat. Indicating Dyce is No RA48 (BWG 93), an Alexander-bodied Leyland PD1 new in July 1948. Route 2 was an hourly weekday service between Banchory and Dyce passing through Aberdeen at Union Terrace. The journey time for the whole route was 1 hour 27 minutes, with 27 minutes between Union Terrace and Dyce. The single fare between Aberdeen and Dyce was 9d.

ABERDEEN Sixteen miles west of Aberdeen is the small town of Kemnay. No P410 (WG 5928), an Alexander-bodied Leyland TS7 new in April 1937, would be one of the last four TS7s to be sold for scrap in December 1963. Route 19 was between Blackfriars Street in Aberdeen and Keig, but most journeys terminated at either Kemnay or Monymusk. The journey time to Kemnay was 45 minutes and the single fare was 1s 8d.

ABERDEEN On Rosemount Viaduct with the indicator set for Alford, 26 miles west of Aberdeen, is No P410 (WG 5928), an Alexander-bodied Leyland TS7 new in April 1937; it would be sold for scrap in December 1963. From Monday to Friday five buses ran from Blackfriars Street in Aberdeen to Alford, with a journey time of 1 hour 18 minutes and a return fare of 5s 0d.

ABERDEEN At the north end of Union Terrace, with Herd's Lugano Café in the background, is No P368 (WG 5507), an Alexander-bodied Leyland TS7 new in March 1937. This vehicle was sold to McGarry of Dumbarton as a mobile shop in April 1960, and would last in that role until June 1962, when it was scrapped.

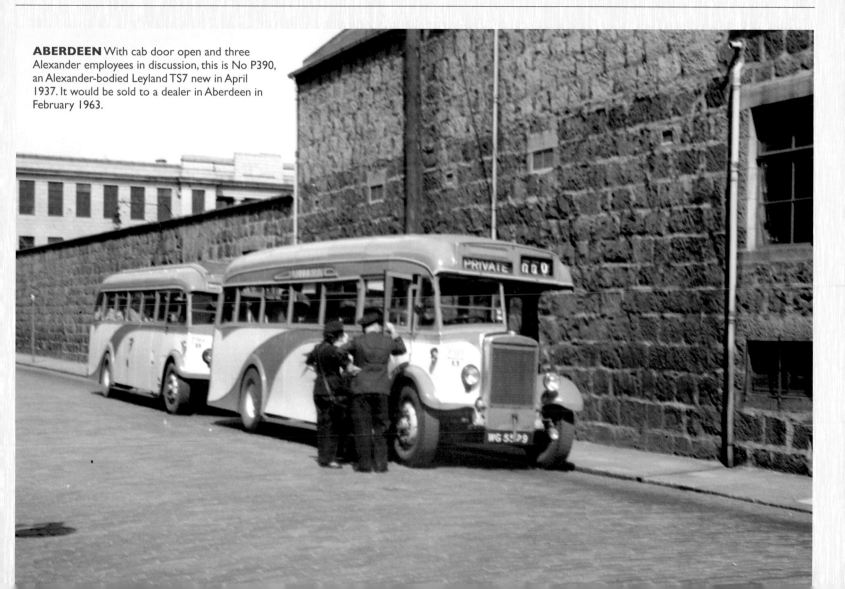

ABERDEEN With cab door open and three Alexander employees in discussion, this is No P390, an Alexander-bodied Leyland TS7 new in April 1937. It would be sold to a dealer in Aberdeen in February 1963.

ABERDEEN Also seen on Rosemount Viaduct is No P384 (WG 5523), an Alexander-bodied Leyland TS7; it was one of a number of Leyland TS7s that survived to be transferred to Alexander Northern in May 1961. This example would be sold to a Glasgow dealer in January 1963.

ABERDEEN The distinctive church in the right background is the North Church, affectionately known locally as the 'Pepper Pot', designed by Aberdeen architect John Smith and opened in June 1831. The bus is No P615 (WG 9008), an Alexander-bodied Leyland TS8 special new in March 1940; all the TS8 specials that passed to Alexander Northern in May 1961 were sold in December 1963 apart from No P671, which had become a caravan in August 1961.

ABERDEEN The fleet of James Sutherland of Peterhead, which was acquired by Alexander in March 1950, included 12 all-Leyland PD1As. Representative of these in Aberdeen is No RA93 (DAV 306), and alongside is No RA90 (DAV 303), both new to Sutherland in May 1947; the former was sold for scrap in January 1970, while the latter was exported to Boston, USA, in January 1971. No RA93 has completed a journey on route 62 between Methlick and Aberdeen, with a journey time of 1 hour 8 minutes for a single fare of 2s 1d.

ABERDEEN With a fair complement of passengers, No RA90 (DAV 303) is seen again soon to leave for 40-miles-plus journey to Rosehearty. During weekdays there were eight return journeys on route 63 between Rosehearty and Aberdeen, increasing to 12 on Saturdays. The journey took 2 hours 13 minutes, the single fare was 4s 3d, and the return 7s 7d.

ABERDEEN Between May 1944 and March 1946 Sutherland took delivery of ten Daimler CWA6s, seven with Duple bodywork, two with Massey bodywork and one with bodywork by Brush. Indicating Ellon, this is No RO686 (CAV 897), one of those with Duple bodywork, new in June 1945. All the Daimler CWA6s passed to Alexander Midland in January 1962, but No RO686 was sold for scrap in March 1964. Although indicating Ellon, no route number is shown; this will be 53A between Aberdeen and Ellon via Balmedie, taking 42 minutes and costing 1s 4d one way.

ABERDEEN Less than a month into service when this view was taken, this is No AC88 (HMS 237), an Alexander-bodied AEC Reliance. Alongside is another of the former Sutherland of Peterhead all-Leyland PD1As, No RA95 (DAV 308). Both are allocated to Peterhead and both are indicated to go to Peterhead by different routes. Route 53 is Aberdeen to Peterhead via Ellon with a journey time of 1½ hours, while route 58 is Aberdeen to Peterhead via Cruden Bay with the same journey time. The single fare was 3s 3d. No RA95 was, like No RA90, exported to Boston, USA, in January 1971, while No AC88 passed to a dealer in Turriff in August 1977.

FALKIRK We have now journeyed south from Aberdeen to Falkirk bus station on 15 August 1956. Nearest the camera is No RC12 (CWG 875), an Alexander-bodied AEC Regent III new in April 1951. In contrast, alongside is No R252 (WG 8676), an all-Leyland TD5 new in June 1939. No RC12 was sold to a dealer in January 1970.

FALKIRK At the parking area at the bus station on the same day is No P592 (WG 8809), an Alexander-bodied Leyland TS8 new in June 1939; it was sold by Alexander Midland in December 1962.

EDINBURGH In 1956 many of the Edinburgh bus and coach services used St Andrew Square for arrivals and departures, while Queen Street, north of St Andrew Square, was used as a parking area for buses and coaches not in service. On 17 August 1956 bus driver and conductor stand in front of their bus, No P531 (WG 8110), an Alexander-bodied Leyland TS8 new in June 1939, which was sold by Alexander in January 1960.

EDINBURGH Queen Street gardens is the background to this view taken on the same day, showing Lawson of Kirkintilloch's No P332 (WG 4446), which was delivered to Alexander in 1936 and first licensed to Simpson's & Forrester's in April 1937, a company acquired by Alexander in February 1938. On receipt of a new Alexander body in April 1949, No P332 passed to Lawson of Kirkintilloch, where it remained until Lawson was absorbed into the Alexander fleet on 1 January 1961. In May 1961 the vehicle passed to Alexander Midland, where it remained until sold in September 1964.

EDINBURGH The last view taken on Queen Street on that August day shows the very new No PD74 (JMS 192), an Alexander-bodied Leyland PSUC1/2.

KIRKCALDY The Esplanade on the seafront is the location of this view taken on 19 August 1956. Nearest the camera is No R149 (WG 5257), an all-Leyland TD4 new in June 1937, which was later acquired by Wright, a showman from Dumfries, in September 1960. Behind, left and right, are two Cravens-bodied Guy Arab IIIs new in 1948. Route 339 indicated by No R149 was between Kirkcaldy Esplanade and Leslie, a frequent service with a journey time of 45 minutes and a single fare of 11d.

KIRKCALDY Even with the sun shining, the presence of a large raincoat would indicate that it is pretty cold on the Esplanade on that August day. The driver is changing the route indicator of Kirkcaldy-allocated No R244 (WG 8263), an all-Leyland TD5 new in March 1939; it would pass to Alexander Fife but was never operated and was sold to a dealer in June 1961. Route 334 was between Kirkcaldy Esplanade and Lochgelly Auchterdorran Road, with a bus every 20 minutes from Monday to Friday. The journey took 35 minutes and the single fare was 11d.

NEWBURGH At the depot on 19 August 1956 are two Alexander-bodied Leyland TS7s, Nos P427 (WG 6416) (right), and P421 (WG 6410); No P421 was new in November 1937 and No P427 a month later. No P421 was sold for scrap in July 1959, while No P427 became a showman's bus in September 1960.

ABERDOUR At the railway station on 22 August 1956 is No PD33 (FWG 179), an Alexander-bodied Leyland PSUC1/2 new to Lawson's in July 1954; it passed to Alexander Midland in May 1961 and remained in the fleet until sold for scrap in June 1970.

Below: **STIRLING** In the bus station indicating Doune is No R271 (WG 9185), an all-Leyland TD7 new in March 1940. This vehicle would be transferred to Alexander Midland in May 1961, remaining in that fleet until sold for scrap in October 1963. Alongside it is No P397 (WG 5536), an Alexander-bodied Leyland TS7 new in April 1937, which was sold in October 1960 and was later noted as a caravan in Beattock five months later. Route 20 was between Glasgow and Callander via Stirling, but a few services indicating route 20 left Stirling for Doune, taking only 30 minutes for the journey for a fare of 10d.

Above: **STIRLING** is 30 miles west of Aberdour, and the following views were taken on 22 August 1956. All four coaches in this view are about to leave Stirling bus station for Edinburgh. Nearest the camera is No PA142 (CMS 211), an Alexander-bodied Leyland PS1 new in October 1949, which passed to Alexander Northern in May 1961 and was sold to T. D. Alexander (Greyhound), Arbroath, in July 1971. Next in line is an Alexander-bodied Leyland PSU1/15 new in 1952, and the last that can be identified is another 1949 Alexander-bodied Leyland PS1.

STIRLING This is No P399 (WG 5538), an Alexander-bodied Leyland TS7 new in April 1937. It was later sold to a dealer in July 1960.

STIRLING Leaving the city for Glasgow is No AC91 (HMS 240), an Alexander-bodied AEC Reliance that was less than a month into service when this picture was taken. It would pass to Alexander Northern in May 1961, remaining in that fleet until sold for scrap in May 1975. Route 21 was the limited-stop service between Dundee and Glasgow Buchanan Street via Stirling bus station; the journey time from Stirling to Glasgow was 1 hour 10 minutes, and between Dundee and Glasgow was just short of 3½ hours.

STIRLING This is No R466 (WG 3386), originally numbered P304, an Alexander-bodied Leyland TS7 new in July 1936. It had received a new Alexander L27/26 body in March 1944 together with an AEC six-cylinder 7.7-litre oil engine, and was renumbered R466. It was sold to a dealer in April 1961.

STIRLING On tour in the city is No PD64 (GWG 290), an Alexander-bodied Leyland PSUC1/1 new in November 1955. This vehicle would pass to Alexander Fife in May 1961 and remain in that fleet until sold to Muir in Kirkcaldy in August 1974.

STIRLING With a heavy exhaust plume, this is No R468 (AFG 682) in Drip Road. New in July 1935 as No P247, an Alexander-bodied Leyland TS7, this bus was acquired by Alexander as part of the large fleet of General Motor Carrying Company of Kirkcaldy in May 1937. It subsequently received a new Alexander L27/26 body and an AEC 7.7-litre oil engine in April 1944, and was renumbered R468. It passed to Greyhound Coaches of Sheffield and Arbroath in August 1960, but had been scrapped by the end of the year.

PERTH Standing outside Alexander's depot in the city on 23 August 1956 is No P717 (VD 3459), a Leyland LT5A that had been new to Central SMT in July 1934. It was acquired through Millburn Motors of Glasgow in August 1945 and received a new Alexander body in October of that year; at the same time it was fitted with an AEC 7.7-litre oil engine. The bus was resold to Millburn Motors in August 1959, and acquired by a showman, being noted as such in Girvan in 1961.

PERTH On the left of this view at the depot is No P715 (VD 3414), a Leyland LT5A new to Lanarkshire Traction Company in June 1934 and acquired by Alexander in October 1945, where it received a new Alexander body and an AEC 7.7-litre oil engine. In the middle is No P709 (WG 3252), an Alexander-bodied Leyland LT5A that was new in March 1935, which received an AEC 7.7-litre oil engine in August 1945. On the right is No P714 (VD 3444), a Leyland LT5A new to Central SMT in July 1934; acquired by Alexander in October 1945, it received a new Alexander body and was also fitted with an AEC 7.7-litre oil engine. No P715 was acquired by Ogilvie of Stirling in January 1958 and was last licensed in 1960. P709 was scrapped by Alexander in November 1979, and P714 was sold in January 1958 and later converted to a shop.

PERTH Standing outside the depot is No P571 (WG 8150), an Alexander-bodied Leyland TS8 new in May 1939; it passed to Alexander Midland in May 1961 but within a few months had been sold to Anderson & Ring, contractors, who scrapped it in March 1962. Alongside No P571 is another of the Leyland LT5As acquired from Central SMT, No P719 (VD 3471), which also received a new Alexander body and an AEC 7.7-litre oil engine in November 1945 before entering service; it was acquired by Greyhound Coaches of Sheffield and Arbroath in July 1958.

PERTH About to disembark a full bus load of passengers is No P573 (WG 8790), an Alexander-bodied Leyland TS8 special new in June 1939. This bus was sold by Alexander Midland in December 1961 and was later noted as a caravan at Tummel Bridge in July 1965.

PERTH Outside the Sandeman Public Library on Kinnoull Street, working city service to Muirton North, is former London Transport No RO723 (HGC 109), a Park Royal-bodied Guy Arab II new in January 1946. Acquired by Alexander in May 1953, it is in the red livery of Perth city services. It was sold for scrap in August 1959.

PERTH Working the City Hall to Hunter Crescent Perth city service is No RO701 (GYL 434), an NCME-bodied Guy Arab II that had been new to London Transport in December 1945. It was acquired by Alexander in March 1953 and ran for that company in the red livery of the Perth city fleet. It was withdrawn in June 1962 and acquired by Northern Roadways that month.

PERTH Standing outside the City Hall is No A8 (AMS 588), a Burlingham-bodied AEC Regal I new in August 1946. It was sold by Alexander Midland to Wight Construction of Grangemouth in July 1964.

PERTH This is No P709 (WG 3252), an Alexander-bodied Leyland LT5A new in March 1935. It had its original Leyland four-cylinder oil engine replaced by an AEC six-cylinder 7.7-litre oil engine in August 1945 and received a new Alexander body in October of that year. The bus was scrapped by Alexander in November 1959.

PERTH At the Station Hotel is No G73 (BMS 843), an all-Guy Arab III new in February 1948. It will soon be departing on route 369 to Cupar, a journey time of just over the hour. The Guy would pass to Alexander Fife in May 1961 and, like many Fife buses, would be sold to Muir of Kirkcaldy for scrap in March 1967.

LARBERT At the back of Larbert depot on 20 September 1956 is No W82 (WG 8471), a Duple-bodied Bedford WTB new in May 1939. This view may be the last taken of this vehicle in Alexander livery as it had been sold to Foster of Arbroath by the end of the month.

LARBERT Route 86 was between Camelon Brown Street and Grangemouth Soap Works via Falkirk with a journey time of 30 minutes. Working an 86 to Kerse Road on 21 September 1956 is Grangemouth-allocated No RO469 (AMS 110), a Brush-bodied Daimler CWA6 new in May 1944. The bus passed to Alexander Midland in May 1961 and was sold to Highland Omnibuses in April 1964, but they never operated it.

FALKIRK Leaving the bus station for Alloa is No AC80 (GWG 484), an Alexander-bodied AEC Monocoach new in July 1955; the journey time between Falkirk bus station and Alloa was 49 minutes. This bus would pass to Alexander Northern in May 1961, where it would remain until sold to Guthrie of Craigo in August 1975.

Appendix Fleet list for buses and coaches that appear in this book, in order of building/acquisition

Fleet numbers	Registration numbers	Chassis	Bodywork	Year new
R44-R49	WG 3378-WG 3383	Leyland TD4	Leyland	1935
P201-P267	WG 3440-WG 3491	Leyland TS7	Alexander	1935

Fleet numbers	Registration numbers	Chassis	Bodywork	Year new
P301-P307	WG 3261 WG 3384-3389	Leyland TS7	Alexander	1936
P308-P327	WG 3492-WG 3511	Leyland TS7	Alexander	1936
R101-R120	WG 4455-WG 4474	Leyland TD4	Leyland	1936
R121-R122	WG 4923-WG 4933	Leyland TD4	Leyland	1936
P334-P337	WG 4448-WG 4451	Leyland TS7	Alexander	1937
R132-R150	WG 4934-WG 4946/WG 5253-WG 5258	Leyland TD4	Leyland	1937
P351-P400	WG 5487-WG 5539 *except* WG 5494/5500/05	Leyland TS7	Alexander	1937
P401-P435	WG 5919-WG 5928/WG 6401-WG 6423/WG 6425	Leyland TS7	Alexander	1937

Above: **DUNFERMLINE** On 10 November 1956, indicating route 306 to Leven, is No R397 (WG 3458). This was originally a single-deck Alexander-bodied Leyland TS7 new in June 1935, then in July 1943 it was rebuilt to Leyland TD4 specification, rebodied with a new Alexander L27/26R body and the 'P' number changed to R397. It was sold for scrap in January 1958. Route 306 was a half-hourly service on Monday to Saturday; the journey from Dunfermline to Leven took 1 hour 50 minutes and cost 2s 6d one-way.

Right: **KIRKCALDY** Standing in the bus station on 30 November 1956 is No P412 (WG 6401), an Alexander-bodied Leyland TS7 new in November 1937; it was withdrawn and sold for scrap September 1960.

The General Motor Carrying Company Ltd of Kirkcaldy was taken over in May 1937. Four of its vehicles appear in the book and their details are given in the text.

Fleet numbers	Registration numbers	Chassis	Bodywork	Year new
K6-K35	WG 7238-WG 7267	Leyland LZ2A	Burlingham	1938
K41-K90	WG 7479-WG 7508/ WG 7630	Leyland LZ2A	Alexander	1938

LOCATION UNKNOWN Working a school journey on 20 August 1956 is No K60 (WG 7498), an Alexander-bodied Leyland LZ2A new in July 1938. It was fitted with a Leyland 7.4-litre oil engine in November 1946, replacing the original petrol engine. In January 1957 this bus was acquired by W. Bellis & Sons, Buckley, remaining in that fleet until February 1959, when it was acquired by a showman in Wakefield.

Simpsons & Forresters of Dunfermline were acquired in February 1938. Some of the company's vehicles appear in the book and their details are given in the text.

Fleet numbers	Registration numbers	Chassis	Bodywork	Year new
K71-K89	WG 7509-WG 7517	Leyland LZ2A	Alexander	1939
	WG 7620-WG 7629	Leyland LZ2A	Alexander	1939
W70	WG 7950	Bedford WTB	Duple	1939
P522-P571	WG 8101-WG 8150	Leyland TS8	Alexander	1939
R230-R249	WG 8249-WG 8268	Leyland TD5	Leyland	1939
K71-K89	WG 7509-WG 7517	Leyland LZ2A	Alexander	1939
	WG 7620-WG 7629	Leyland LZ2A	Alexander	1939
W70	WG 7950	Bedford WTB	Duple	1939
P522-P571	WG 8101-WG 8150	Leyland TS8	Alexander	1939
R230-R249	WG 8249-WG 8268	Leyland TD5	Leyland	1939
W71-W72	WG 8613-WG 8614	Bedford WTB	Duple	1939
R250-R257	WG 8674-WG 8681	Leyland TD5	Leyland	1939
P572-P596	WG 8789-WG 8813	Leyland TS8SP	Alexander	1939

KIRKCALDY At the depot on 20 June 1956 is No P585 (WG 8802), an Alexander-bodied Leyland TS8 special new in June 1939. It was transferred to Alexander Fife in May 1961 and scrapped six months later.

ANSTRUTHER Working a school journey from Anstruther depot on 20 July 1956 is No R283 (WG 9197), an all-Leyland TD7 new in March 1940. The bus passed to Alexander Midland in May 1961 and was acquired by Sutherland Police in August 1963 as a safety demonstration vehicle, remaining as such until sold for scrap in June 1971.

Fleet numbers	Registration numbers	Chassis	Bodywork	Year new
P597	WG 8990	Leyland TS8SP	Alexander	1939
P600	WG 8993	Leyland TS8SP	Alexander	1939
P648-P649	WG 8479-WG 8480	Leyland TS8SP	Alexander	1940
P598-P599	WG 8991-WG 8992	Leyland TS8SP	Alexander	1940
P601-P621	WG 8994-WG 9014	Leyland TS8SP	Alexander	1940
R266-R290	WG 9180-WG 9204	Leyland TD7	Leyland	1940

Fleet numbers	Registration numbers	Chassis	Bodywork	Year new
P628-P643	WG 9318-WG 9333	Leyland TS8SP	Alexander	1940
P650-P682	WG 9486-WG 9518	Leyland TS8SP	Alexander	1940
R312	WG 9519	Leyland TD7	Leyland	1941
R314-R321	WG 9543-WG 9550	Leyland TD7	Leyland	1941

Fleet numbers	Registration numbers	Chassis	Bodywork	Year new
R328-R329	WG 9631-WG 9632	Leyland TD7	Leyland	1941
R331-R332	WG 9634-WG 9635	Leyland TD7	Leyland	1941
R333	WG 9642	Leyland TD7	Leyland	1942
R334-R335	WG 9724-WG 9725	Leyland TD7	Leyland	1942
P684-P685	WG 9754-WG 9755	Leyland TS11	Willowbrook	1942
RO439	WG 9819	Guy Arab I	Duple	1942
RO440-RO441	WG 9820-WG 9821	Guy Arab I	Strachan	1943
RO442	WG 9884	Guy Arab I	NCME	1943
RO443-RO444	WG 9921-WG 9922	Guy Arab I	Strachan	1943
RO455	AMS 42	Guy Arab II	Roe	1944
RO459-RO462	AMS 46-AMS 49	Guy Arab II	Roe	1944
RO469-RO471	AMS 110-AMS 112	Daimler CWA6	Brush	1944
RO472-RO475	AMS 114-AMS 147	Guy Arab II	NCME	1944
RO476	AMS 148	Guy Arab II	Roe	1944
RO477-RO491	AMS 149-AMS 163	Guy Arab II	NCME	1944
RO492-RO496	AMS 182-AMS 186	Guy Arab II	NCME	1944
RO497-RO501	AMS 187-AMS 191	Guy Arab II	Roe	1944

LOCHGELLY Photographed at the depot on 2 October 1956, this is No RO497 (AMS 187), a Roe-bodied Guy Arab II new in September 1944. It is indicating route 334, Kirkcaldy to Lochgelly, which had a journey time of 35 minutes for a single fare of 11d. This bus was scrapped in October 1962.

Fleet numbers	Registration numbers	Chassis	Bodywork	Year new
RO502	AMS 209	Guy Arab II	Roe	1944
RO514-RO523	AMS 229-AMS 238	Guy Arab II	NCME	1944
RO524-RO532	AMS 270-AMS 278	Guy Arab II	NCME	1944
RO544-RO545	AMS 7-AMS 8	Guy Arab II	WEYMANN	1945
RO503-RO513	AMS 210-AMS 220	Guy Arab II	NCME	1945
RO533	AMS 279	Guy Arab II	NCME	1945

Fleet numbers	Registration numbers	Chassis	Bodywork	Year new
RO534-RO539	AMS 309-AMS 314	Guy Arab II	NCME	1945
RO540-RO543	AMS 315-AMS 318	Guy Arab II	Weymann	1945

Above: **LOCHGELLY** At the depot on 2 October 1956 is No RO542 (AMS 317), a Weymann-bodied Guy Arab II from June 1945. It passed to Alexander Fife in May 1961 and remained in that fleet until sold for scrap in December 1965.

Above right: **KIRKCALDY** At the depot on 2 June 1956 is No RO543 (AMS 318), another of the same batch new in June 1945. It was sold for scrap in February 1963.

Acquired from Lanarkshire Traction Company in 1945

Fleet numbers	Registration numbers	Chassis	Bodywork	Year new
P715	VD 3414	Leyland LT5A	Alexander	1934
P716	VD 3421	Leyland LT5A	Alexander	1934
P718	VD 3411	Leyland LT5A	Alexander	1934

Acquired from Central SMT, Motherwell, in 1945

Fleet numbers	Registration numbers	Chassis	Bodywork	Year new
P714	VD 3444	Leyland LT5A	Alexander	1934
P717	VD 3459	Leyland LT5A	Alexander	1934
P719	VD 3471	Leyland LT5A	Alexander	1934
P720	VD 3469	Leyland LT5A	Alexander	1934
P721-P722	VD 3433-VD 3434	Leyland LT5A	Alexander	1934

LOCATION UNKNOWN Seen on 3 April 1956 is No R551 (JY 5002), a Leyland TD4 that had been new to Plymouth Corporation in February 1935 and was acquired by Alexander in July 1945; it was fitted with new Alexander bodywork and entered service in January 1946. No R551 survived to pass to Alexander Fife in May 1961 but was scrapped a month later.

Acquired from Plymouth Corporation in 1945

Fleet numbers	Registration numbers	Chassis	Bodywork	Year new
R546-R557	JY 6732/JY 5034/ JY 5002/ JY 5004/ JY 6737/JY 5020/ JY 5014/JY 5332/ JY 6756/JY 5025/JY 5006AI	Leyland TD4	Weymann (R546-548/551-557 New Alexander bodywork in 1946)	1934-1936
	JY 3654	Leyland TD4	Weymann	

Right: **ABERHILL** Also seen on 3 April 1956 is No PA27 (AWG 702), one of the first batch of Alexander-bodied Leyland PS1s delivered new in May 1947. This bus would be more than 20 years old when it was sold for scrap in February 1968.

Fleet numbers	Registration numbers	Chassis	Bodywork	Year ne
A11-A20	AMS 486-AMS 495	AEC Regal I	Burlingham	1946
A21-A30	AMS 496-AMS 505	AEC Regal I	Alexander	1946
G1-G3	AMS 531-AMS 533	Guy Arab III	Duple	1946
G31-G40	AMS 561-AMS 570	Guy Arab III	Massey	1946
R611-R616	AWB 929/AWB 942 AWB 944/AWB 945/ AWB 949/AWB 950	Leyland TD3	Cravens	1934
R617	CWB 72	Leyland TD4	Cravens	1936
R618	CWB 74	Leyland TD4	Cravens	1936
R619	CWB 981	Leyland TD4	Cravens	1936
R620	CWB 986	Leyland TD4	Cravens	1936
R621	BWE 34	Leyland TD4	Cravens	1935
R622	BWE 40	Leyland TD4	Cravens	1935

R614/616-619 were not operated by Alexander

Fleet numbers	Registration numbers	Chassis	Bodywork	Year new
A1-A10	AMS 581-AMS 590	AEC Regal I	Burlingham	1946
RA7	AMS 4	Leyland PD1	Alexander	1947
G4-G10	AMS 534-AMS 540	Guy Arab III	Duple	1947
G49	AMS 579	Guy Arab III	Alexander	1947
PA1-PA25	AWG 536-AWG 560	Leyland PS1	Alexander	1947
A31-A65	AWG 618-AWG 652	AEC Regal I	Alexander	1947
PA26-PA39	AWG 701-AWG 714	Leyland PS1	Alexander	1947
R608	AWG 715	Leyland PD1	Burlingham	1947
D1	AWG 896	Daimler CVD6	Burlingham	1947
W201-W202	AWG 992-AWG 993	Bedford OB	SMT	1947
A66-A75	BMS 100-BMS 109	AEC Regal I	Burlingham	1947
AA1-AA10	BMS 110-BMS 119	AEC Regal III	Burlingham	1947
RA6	BMS 201	Leyland PD1	Alexander	1947
PA40-PA48	BMS 202-BMS 20	Leyland PS1	Alexander	1947
PA59	BMS 221	Leyland PS1	Alexander	1947
R610	BMS 313	Leyland PD1	Burlingham	1947
RO574	CST 5	Guy Arab II	NCME	1947

Vehicles acquired from W. Greig of Inverness in 1947 and operated

Fleet numbers	Registration numbers	Chassis	Bodywork	Year new
RO569	AST 959	Guy Arab II	Roe	1944
RO570	BST 31	Guy Arab II	NCME	1945
RO571	BST 53	Guy Arab II	NCME	1945
RO572	BST 171	Guy Arab II	NCME	1946

Vehicles acquired from Sheffield Corporation in 1947 and operated

Fleet numbers	Registration numbers	Chassis	Bodywork	Year new
R622	BWE 40	Leyland TD4	Cravens	1935
RA8-RA12	AMS 5/AMS 9-AMS 12	Leyland PD1	Alexander	1948
G41-G50	AMS 571-AMS 580	Guy Arab III	Brockhouse	1948
RA13-RA30	AWG 351-AWG 368	Leyland PD1	Alexander	1948
RO583-RO607	AWG 369-AWG 393	Guy Arab III	Cravens	1948
G51-G60	AWG 565-AWG 573	Guy Arab III	Brockhouse	1948

Right: **KIRKCALDY** In October 1947 the 20-vehicle fleet of W. Greig of Inverness was acquired by Alexander. Only four Guy Arab IIs entered service with Alexander, together with one Guy Arab II ordered by Greig but delivered to Alexander in December 1947. On the right of this view at the depot on 3 May 1956 is No RO569 (AST 959), with Roe bodywork when new in May 1944; it was sold for scrap by Alexander Fife in August 1962. Next in line are two former London Guy Arab IIs, then three Leyland TDs.

Fleet numbers	Registration numbers	Chassis	Bodywork	Year new
W213-W215	BMS 97-BMS 99	Bedford OB	SMT	1948
PA49-PA58	BMS 211-BMS 220	Leyland PS1	Alexander	1948
RA5	BMS 316	Leyland PD1	Burlingham	1948
D2-D30	BMS 397-BMS 425	Daimler CVD6	Burlingham	1948
A76-A82	BMS 462-BMS 468	AEC Regal I	Burlingham	1948
G62-G71	BMS 584-BMS 593	Guy Arab III	Massey	1948
PA61-PA75	BMS 688-BMS 702	Leyland PS1	Alexander	1948
G72-G101	BMS 842-BMS 871	Guy Arab III	Guy	1948
W216-W222	BMS 931-BMS 932/ BWG 39-BWG 43	Bedford OB	SMT	1948

Fleet numbers	Registration numbers	Chassis	Bodywork	Year new
W216-W222	BMS 931-BMS 932/ BWG 39-BWG 43	Bedford OB	SMT	1948
RA31-RA60	BWG 76-BWG 105	Leyland PD1	Alexander	1948
W229-W233	BWG 244-BWG 248	Bedford OB	SMT	1948
PA76-PA100	BWG 302-BWG 326	Leyland PS1	Alexander	1948
G61	BMS 595	Guy Arab III	Brockhouse	1949
PA101-PA124	BWG 506-BWG 529	Leyland PS1	Alexander	1949
W236	BWG 540	Bedford OB	Duple	1949
D31-D35	BWG 570-BWG 574	Daimler CVD6	Burlingham	1949
W234	BWG 983	Bedford OB	Duple	1949
C1-C7	CMS 2-CMS 8	Commer	Scottish AV	1949
W235	CMS 47	Bedford OB	Duple	1949
W237	CMS 103	Bedford OB	Duple	1949
PA126-PA144	CMS 194-CMS 213	Leyland PS1	Alexander	1949
C14-C28	CMS 286-CMS 300	Commer	Scottish AV	1949
W238	CMS 316	Bedford OB	Duple	1949
RA61-RA64	CMS 364-CMS 367	Leyland PD1	Alexander	1949

LOCATION UNKNOWN This view of No G100 (BMS 870), a Guy-bodied Guy Arab III new in February 1948, was taken on 3 April 1956. The indicator shows route 302, a 19-minute journey between Dunfermline and Rosyth Docks. No G100 would be sold for scrap by Alexander Fife in December 1963.

Vehicles transferred from SMT in December 1949

Fleet numbers	Registration numbers	Chassis	Bodywork	Year new
P823	SC 3352	Leyland TS2	Alexander	1929
P807	SC 4370	Leyland TS2	Alexander	1929
P808-P814	ASF 365-ASF 371	Leyland TS7	Alexander	1937
P824	ASF 372	Leyland TS7	Alexander	1937
P825-P826	ASF 377-ASF 378	Leyland TS7	Alexander	1937
P827-P828	ASF 381-ASF 382	Leyland TS7	Alexander	1937
P829	ASF 384	Leyland TS7	Alexander	1937
P837-P839	ASF 388-ASF 390	Leyland TS7	Alexander	1937
P815	ASF 395	Leyland TS7	Alexander	1937
K91-K105	BSC 501-BSC 515	Leyland LZ2A	Alexander	1938
P816-P818	CSF 224-CSF 226	Leyland TS8	Alexander	1939
P819	CSF 231	Leyland TS8	Alexander	1939
P840	CSF 232	Leyland TS8	Alexander	1939
P820-P821	CSF 233-CSF 234	Leyland TS8	Alexander	1939
P830-P832	CSF 236-CSF 238	Leyland TS8	Alexander	1939
P833-P836	CSF 240-CSF 243	Leyland TS8	Alexander	1939
P822	CSF 244	Leyland TS8	Alexander	1939
P841-P842	CSF 245-CSF 246	Leyland TS8	Alexander	1939
P843-P844	CSF 250-CSF 251	Leyland TS8	Alexander	1939
P845-P846	CSF 253-CSF 254	Leyland TS8	Alexander	1939
PA196	AWG 591	Leyland PS1	Alexander	1950
PA194-PA195	BMS 314-BMS 315	Leyland PS1	Alexander	1950
PA145	CMS 214	Leyland PS1	Alexander	1950

Fleet numbers	Registration numbers	Chassis	Bodywork	Year new
PA146-PA160	CWG 28-CWG 42	Leyland PS1	Alexander	1950
RB65-RB89	CWG 43-CWG 67	Leyland PD2/1	Alexander	1950
PA161-PA166	CWG 203-CWG 208	Leyland PS1	Alexander	1950
BA1-BA5	CWG 226-CWG 230	Albion FT3AB	Strachan	1950
PA167-PA193	CWG 269-CWG 295	Leyland PS1	Alexander	1950
RB102-RB103	CWG 296-CWG 297	Leyland PD2/1	Alexander	1950
PA203-PA216	CWG 330-CWG 343	Leyland PS1	Burlingham	1950

LOCHGELLY The last Leyland PS1s delivered new to Alexander were bodied by Burlingham and delivered in July 1950. Representing this batch at Lochgelly depot on 2 October 1956 is No PA213 (CWG 340), which was one of five of the Burlingham-bodied Leyland PS1s transferred to Alexander Fife and was scrapped by that company in June 1965.

Fleet numbers	Registration numbers	Chassis	Bodywork	Year new
RB104	CWG 632	Leyland PD2/1	Alexander	1950

Vehicles acquired from J. Sutherland of Peterhead on 1 March 1950 and operated

Fleet numbers	Registration numbers	Chassis	Bodywork	Year new
A91	AV 9467	AEC Regal	Duple	1937
R663-R664	AV 9962-AV 9963	Leyland TD5	Leyland	1937
A93	AAV 844	AEC Regal	Duple	1938
RO672	CAV 3	Guy Arab II	NCME	1943
RO673-RO674	CAV 14-CAV 15	Guy Arab II	NCME	1943
RO675	CAV 122	Guy Arab II	Pickering	1943
RO676	CAV 170	Guy Arab II	NCME	1943
RO677	CAV 175	Guy Arab II	NCME	1943
RO678-RO679	CAV 237-CAV 238	Guy Arab II	NCME	1944
RO680	CAV 243	Guy Arab II	NCME	1944
RO681	CAV 314	Daimler CWA6	Brush	1944
RO682	CAV 595	Daimler CWA6	Duple	1944
RO683-RO685	CAV 824-CAV 826	Daimler CWA6	Duple	1945
RO686-RO688	CAV 897-CAV 899	Daimler CWA6	Duple	1945
AL2	CSA 155	Albion CX13	Walker	1946

Fleet numbers	Registration numbers	Chassis	Bodywork	Year new
RO689-RO690	CSA 342-CSA 343	Daimler CWA6	Massey	1946
RA90-RA95	DAV 303-DAV 308	Leyland PD1A	Leyland	1947
A94-A97	DSA 113-DSA 116	AEC Regal	Brush	1947
RA96-RA101	DSA 848-853	Leyland PD1A	Leyland	1948
RO670	EAV 161	Albion CX19	Walker	1948
PA197-PA200	EAV 458-EAV 461	Leyland PS1	Duple	1948
P201	EAV 636	Leyland PS1	Duple	1948
PA202	ESA 205	Leyland PS1	Duple	1949
RO692-RO693	FAV 826-FAV 827	AEC Regent III	Massey	1949

Vehicles acquired from Wemyss Bros, Ardersier, on 26 June 1950 and operated

Fleet numbers	Registration numbers	Chassis	Bodywork	Year new
RO694	BST 57	Guy Arab II	Roe	1945
RO695	CST 671	CROSSLEY DD42/5Roe	1947	
RC1-RC20	CWG 864-CWG 883	AEC Regent III	Alexander	1951
A99-A104	DMS 125-DMS 130	AEC Regal III	Alexander	1951
RB106-RB117	DMS 340-DMS 351	Leyland PD2/12	Alexander	1951
RB118	DMS 476	Leyland PD2/3	Alexander	1951

Fleet numbers	Registration numbers	Chassis	Bodywork	Year new
RB119-RB144	DMS 479-DMS 504	Leyland PD2/3	Alexander	1951
D36-D48	DMS 549-DMS 561	Daimler CVD6	ECW	1951
PC1	BMS 222	Leyland PSU1/15	Alexander	1952
PC2-PC22	CMS 368-CMS 388	Leyland PSU1/15	Alexander	1952
PC23	CMS 920	Leyland PSU1/15	Alexander	1952
PC24	CWG 298	Leyland PSU1/15	Alexander	1952

Fleet numbers	Registration numbers	Chassis	Bodywork	Year new
PB1-PB20	DMS 814-DMS 833	Leyland OPS2/1	Alexander	1952
PC25-PC27	DWG 521-DWG 523	Leyland PSU1/15	Alexander	1952
PC28-PC33	DWG 524-DWG 529	Leyland PSU1/15	Leyland	1952
PC34-PC37	DWG 691-DWG 694	Leyland PSU1/15	Leyland	1952
PC38-PC41	DWG 771-DWG 774	Leyland PSU1/15	Alexander	1952
PC42-PC43	DWG 805-DWG 806	Leyland PSU1/15	Alexander	1952

EDINBURGH On 20 September 1956 we see No PC24 (CWG 298), an Alexander-bodied Leyland PSU1/15 new in May 1952. It subsequently passed to Alexander Midland, where it remained until sold for scrap in July 1970.

Vehicles acquired from D. Lawson of Kirkintilloch

Fleet numbers	Registration numbers	Chassis	Bodywork	Year new
K1	SN 8847	Leyland LZ2A	Alexander	1938
K36-K40	SN 8558-SN 8562	Leyland LZ2A	Alexander	1938

Vehicles acquired from London Transport

Fleet numbers	Registration numbers	Chassis	Bodywork	Year new
RO631	GYL 307	Guy Arab II	NCME	1945
RO632	GYL 310	Guy Arab II	NCME	1945
RO633	GYL 381	Guy Arab II	NCME	1945
RO635	GYL 383	Guy Arab II	NCME	1945
RO646	HGC 150	Guy Arab II	Weymann	1945
RO636	HGC 157	Guy Arab II	Weymann	1945

Fleet numbers	Registration numbers	Chassis	Bodywork	Year new
RO637	HGC 158	Guy Arab II	Weymann	1945
RO647	HGC 159	Guy Arab II	Weymann	1945
RO640	HGC 166	Guy Arab II	Weymann	1945
RO638	HGC 185	Guy Arab II	Weymann	1945
RO645	HGC 186	Guy Arab II	Weymann	1945
RO643	HGC 193	Guy Arab II	Weymann	1945
RO639	HGC 202	Guy Arab II	Weymann	1945
RO644	HGC 203	Guy Arab II	Weymann	1945
Note: GYL 382, HGC 154 and HGC 188 do not appear in the fleet list as they were withdrawn in 1952.				
RB145-RB167	DWG 901-DWG 923	Leyland PD2/12	Alexander	1953
PC44-PC55	EMS 162-EMS 173	Leyland PSU1/15	Alexander	1953
PC56-PC84	EMS 511-EMS 539	Leyland PSU1/15	Alexander	1953
W241-W252	EMS 824-EMS 835	Bedford SB	Burlingham	1953

Vehicles acquired from London Transport in 1953

Fleet numbers	Registration numbers	Chassis	Bodywork	Year new
RO706	GLF 669	Guy Arab I	Park Royal	1942
RO696	GLL 566	Guy Arab I	Park Royal	1943
RO707	GXE 541	Guy Arab II	Park Royal	1944
RO705	GXE 557	Guy Arab II	Park Royal	1944
RO708	GYE 90	Guy Arab II	Park Royal	1945

KIRKCALDY At the depot in the red livery of the Kirkcaldy town service on 28 June 1956 is No RO705 (GXE 557), a Park Royal-bodied Guy Arab II new to London Transport in February 1944 and acquired by Alexander in March 1953. It was sold for scrap in August 1959. In comparison, to the right is No R149 (WG 5257), an all-Leyland TD4 new in 1937, while to the left is No RO595 (AWG 381), a Cravens-bodied Guy Arab III new in March 1948.

KIRKCALDY Also at the depot on the same day is No RO708 (GYE 90), a Park Royal-bodied Guy Arab II new to London Transport in July 1945 and acquired by Alexander in March 1953. It is also in the red livery of the Kirkcaldy town service and remained as such until sold for scrap in August 1959.

Fleet numbers	Registration numbers	Chassis	Bodywork	Year new
RO698	GYE 91	Guy Arab II	Park Royal	1945
RO709	GYE 92	Guy Arab II	Park Royal	1945
RO699	GYE 95	Guy Arab II	Park Royal	1945
RO710	GYE 96	Guy Arab II	Park Royal	1945
RO721	GYL 337	Guy Arab II	Park Royal	1945
RO711	GYL 431	Guy Arab II	NCME	1945
RO700	GYL 432	Guy Arab II	NCME	1945
RO717	GYL 433	Guy Arab II	NCME	1945

Fleet numbers	Registration numbers	Chassis	Bodywork	Year new
RO701	GYL 434	Guy Arab II	NCME	1945
RO703	GYL 436	Guy Arab II	NCME	1945
RO718	GYL 437	Guy Arab II	NCME	1945
RO712-RO713	GYL 438-GYL 439	Guy Arab II	NCME	1945
RO714	GYL 441	Guy Arab II	NCME	1946
RO702	GYL 444	Guy Arab II	NCME	1946
RO719-RO720	GYL 448-GYL 449	Guy Arab II	NCME	1946
RO704	GYL 450	Guy Arab II	NCME	1946
RO715	GYL 451	Guy Arab II	NCME	1946
RO723	HGC 109	Guy Arab II	Park Royal	1946
RO727	HGC 111	Guy Arab II	Park Royal	1946
RO729	HGC 119	Guy Arab II	Park Royal	1946
RO730	HGC 126	Guy Arab II	Park Royal	1946
RO724	HGC 128	Guy Arab II	Park Royal	1946
RO731	HGC 129	Guy Arab II	Park Royal	1946
RO722	HGC 135	Guy Arab II	Park Royal	1946
RO732	HGC 211	Guy Arab II	Park Royal	1946

Note: RO725 and RO728 do not appear in the fleet list as they were withdrawn in 1954.

PD1-PD19	FMS 718-FMS 736	Leyland PSUC1/2	Alexander	1954
PD23	FMS 740	Leyland PSUC1/2	Alexander	1954
PD25-PD30	FMS 742-FMS 747	Leyland PSUC1/2	Alexander	1954
AC11-AC20	FMS 758-FMS 767	AEC Reliance	Park Royal	1954

Fleet numbers	Registration numbers	Chassis	Bodywork	Year new
AC21-AC30	FMS 977-FMS 986	AEC Monocoach	Park Royal	1954
AC31-AC40	FWG 33-FWG 40	AEC Monocoach	Park Royal	1954
PD31-PD32	FWG 177-FWG 178	Leyland PSUC1/2	Alexander	1954
PD34-PD40	FWG 180-FWG 186	Leyland PSUC1/2	Alexander	1954
AC41-AC42	FMS 738-FMS 739	AEC Reliance	Alexander	1955
AC1-AC10	FMS 748-FMS 757	AEC Reliance	Alexander	1955
E1-E20	FWG 836-FWG 855	Bristol LS6G	ECW	1955
GA1-GA10	GMS 411-GMS 420	Guy Arab LUF	Alexander	1955
AC43-AC50	GWG 94-GWG 101	AEC Reliance	Alexander	1955
PD41-PD70	GWG 267-GWG 296	Leyland PSUC1/2	Alexander	1955
AC51-AC80	GWG 455-GWG 484	AEC Monocoach	Alexander	1955
RA1-RA2	HMS 217-HMS 218	Leyland PD1	Alexander	1955
RA5	HMS 219	Leyland PD1	Alexander	1955
RD1-RD15	GWG 977-GWG 991	Bristol LD6G	ECW	1956
W253-W262	HMS 220-HMS 229	Bedford SBG	Burlingham	1956
AC81-AC97	HMS 230-HMS 246	AEC Reliance	Alexander	1956
AC98-AC99	JMS 49-JMS 50	AEC Reliance	Alexander	1956
PD71-PD100	JMS 189-JMS 218	Leyland PSUC1/2	Alexander	1956

Above: **KIRKCALDY** Seen at the depot on 1 July 1956 is No AC59 (GWG 463), an Alexander-bodied AEC Monocoach new in July 1955. The Monocoach was introduced in 1954 and remained in production until 1958, by which time 359 had been produced – Alexander had 50 delivered new in July 1954 and July 1955. No AC59 passed to Alexander Northern in May 1961 and was sold for scrap in August 1975.

Right: **BETWEEN LEVEN AND KIRKCALDY** Working route 308 on 20 September 1956 is No RD9 (GWG 985), an ECW-bodied Bristol LD6G new in July 1956. Route 308 between Leven and Kirkcaldy was a 40-minute journey and a bus left Leven every 45 minutes. No RD9 was broken up for spares by Alexander Fife in 1971.

Index